AF230174

It all started when
I Married Satan…

Here is the Preface to that book and keep reading to see where we left off and how we got to this new stage of life and book

Maybe it was because I was sexually abused from at least the age of fourteen and down through my younger years (the earliest I remember is five) by not one but five different people who were supposed to be looked at as family (it is a secret that will be taken to my grave if I haven't already told you); or maybe because I felt unloved and wanted attention. Maybe because I didn't feel good about myself because I was told that I looked like a duck and called butter ball when I hit puberty and started developing breast, hips and a big butt; Maybe it was because I watched my grandfather get so drunk that he would fall down the steps (thank God he got delivered from alcohol a demon that played all sides of my family-yep a generational curse). Or maybe because I had created jealousy of my little brother because he always got the new in style clothes and I always had to share my clothes with my mother (until I got old enough to buy them for myself); Maybe it was because I was always being compared to other cousins and had to share barrettes and hair do's. Maybe it was just because I had to take a bath in the same bath water that my mother did right after she got out of the tub; Or maybe it was because I felt that my mother hated the fact that I was born, ruined her life and caused her to miss out on so much of her own life; Maybe it was because I always felt like I was just taking up space in this world since I always felt like a second class citizen squatting; or maybe because I cried myself to sleep and contemplated suicide only for my brother to talk me out of OD'n on pills and/or slitting my wrist; Maybe it was just because my father never came around and didn't want me; and my stepfather physically abused my mother, eventually giving me my first black eye and nose bleed; Or just maybe because the guy who I gave my virginity to (*not really even knowing I was a virgin or how to be one because of the sexual abuse*), made me feel embarrassed because he said that I was "*tight*", and not in the good slang way.

Whatever it was… When I jumped into getting married I saw it as a way of escape, yet I didn't realize how serious of a situation I was getting into. I had gotten married when I shouldn't have…too soon and not in God's biblical order for my life. Although, if I hadn't, I may not have written this book, gained a real testimony, or learned my purpose in life. From the verbal, mental, emotional, spiritual, and physical abuse, I became an even more damaged woman. The devil had already left his bags in my life and I suppressed issues. Issues that would mess up just about every romantic relationship that I would have, cause me to attract the wrong type of man *to* me, and settle for them and their issues.
I had become a woman who became afraid to be alone because of the dependency developed by my ex ___________ (husband, supposed to be husband, thought to be husband –you fill in the blanks).

It scared off guys no matter how good or bad for me they were. Tyler Perry said it best-"some people are in your life for a season and some for a lifetime". I sometimes wonder how many potential lifetimes, I had pushed away and conversely how many seasons I kept around way too long.

I had people at churches where I attended ignore situations at hand, and even my family thought that I was the CRAZY one in my marriage. The more I cried out, the more the devil had pulled the covers over their eyes-everyone's eyes-even mine and pretty much caused me to want to leave this world sooner than God had planned for me to- again.

I once heard someone say that the devil will use someone close to you to hurt you…and that's what I always found to be true. The more I thought about it, the more I had to get my mind reconditioned. I had to work harder than most not to totally lose my mind.

Thanks be to God who had my life's purpose in His hands and gave me time to realize Him and His purpose for me. I see now that I had to go through an abusive marriage and the situations that occurred from it because of all of the people God has sent my way since this has happened. I was like the woman in the Bible who had the issue of blood and had to press her way through a crowd of people to see Jesus. My blood issue was life and my crowd was life's circumstances. Yet, Jesus was there all along and welcomed me into His loving arms, time and time again.

WOW! Over a four and a half year time span, I had been homeless, evicted from almost every residence I had called home --three different places,; used for the little bit of money that I did come across; hungry; smoking cigarettes and "blacks", weed, and drinking; felt lonely and like I didn't fit in; I contemplated suicide; I was depressed, felt worthless; disrespected, angry, violent, desperate, called vulnerable and gullible I experienced three house raids within six months in 2005 (still not totally sure why). I had to deal with shyster types of landlords, lost two cars, been in debt, been to visit people in and out of prisons, cried off and on, I felt like I was in a whirlwind. I came within feet of a dead body just off the machines in the hospital not in a casket and I lived in a house with not one but two cremated bodies in a box. I attracted men who really didn't care about me and often lied saying that they loved and cared about me and to top it all off, I was unattached from a church so I church *hop'd* and I could say so much more but… Just to become a completely whole woman now….**Thank you God!**

Oh!
Is That Why I'm Still Single?

LaDonna M. Smith

Fire and Words Publishing™
A subsidiary of Philatonian Productions

Dedicated to *every man* who has ever been in my life in any capacity.

You have ALL influenced me.

I lived,

I learned,

&

I listened.

Cover design by: LaDonna M. Smith

Forewords by fellow authors: Matthew Bacchus and Darrell R. Freeman, Jr.

Library of Congress Control Number: 2014921626

Data: Smith, LaDonna Montrue

Published by: Fire and Words Publishing™ – a subsidiary of Philatonian Productions ™

Oh! Is That Why I'm Still Single? / by LaDonna M. Smith

FAM029000
Summary:
1. Relationships & Dating
2. Self Help
3. Family
4. Mate Seeking

ISBN 13: 978-1-4951-3546-0

ISBN 10: 1-4951-3546-0

Forewords

It is so ironic and somewhat scary how on point this book is. I actually wrote the book; set it aside and then contacted both of these individuals to write the foreword and nope they had not seen the book. That's right my two fellow authors who wrote the forewords to this book did not see this book until I sent them a completed draft of the manuscript which included their forewords.

From the Mouths of Men

First things first, a woman shouldn't settle or lower her standards. Secondly, we [men] are turned on by sight so there must be an attraction. A woman that is *"put together"* on the outside is a must. She must look good (because like I said we as men are turned on by sight), and after we have gotten our *foot in the door*, we will begin to see who you really are. But as a woman, you have to be careful because once again we are already turned on by sight. You have to know (and learn how to differentiate between) if we are only interested in your physical [body] or if we want to get to know more of you mentally, emotionally and spiritually.

<u>Know who you are.</u> You're more than your physical so don't settle for a man who is only interested in sex. Know who you are and what you won't tolerate.

<u>What does a man want.</u> A man wants love, loyalty and respect. He wants to be appreciated for what he does. Men will show their love through their actions rather than words. We are a work in progress. If you love us through the process then you will celebrate our progress. Some men want and desire a woman who can hold her own. A man doesn't want to feel as if his woman can take care of herself and that she is taking all of his money. In other words, she ought to contribute, and bring something to the table. For an example: pay for dinner. While dating, all the man knows is your physical. Make sure he knows that there is more to you than that. Certainly don't stay around if he is not serious about you. Remember that there is more to you than the natural eyes can see.

<u>Some men are better friends of yours than lovers to you.</u> For those who have started out as friends you may have an advantage over someone else who is meeting their person for the first time and all they see is their physical. The man, who has been friends with a woman before dating, knows some or little about her, and [if] he has made the choice to pursue her in hopes of being with her, and vice versa for the woman. A man or woman won't waste time with someone who isn't a potential boyfriend of girlfriend leading to marriage. I believe it's key that you investigate, ask the important questions [that you will need to ask in order to get all of the necessary information that you need to get]. Learn all you need to learn so you will know if you want to continue *seeing* that person [know when enough is enough]. Many [people] make the mistake of continuing to *see* a person because the person looks good (for those who have given up the physical already while dating) because the sex is good.

<u>To sum it all up.</u> While dating, you should be taking your time. Get to know the person, and communication is the key.

Matthew Bacchus,
Author of
My Poetry, My Story, My Testimony, For His Glory

The Role of Men in Society?
{Is being overlooked by our lack of commitment}

I'm so disgusted by our lack of commitment to our spouse and our children. From the beginning of time we were the providers, and the protectors. We were actively involved in society, the civil rights marches, politics, business, and at home. Sad to say with the change that time brought, it also brought separation. It turned family members against each other.

So many men have walked out on their families, leaving the mothers to be the mother and the father; often finding it difficult [for the women] to teach their boys how to be men. What do they do when their son finally ask those questions like: *Where my daddy at? Why you so hard on me with the "respect women" lectures. And [yet you tell me to] appreciate [and respect] them [women] when my own father turned his back on me and you? Why should I be a man when he didn't have to?*

Women face these issues every day [and] our kids are lacking a father to teach them about life and to protect their family. So women learn to be independent because they have no [other] choice. For so long they have been taking care of their family on their own; replacing the men in society and ultimately throwing us by the wayside [But not all men are bad].

Now on the other hand, there are active fathers and active men in society. So many times their accomplishments are overlooked by *dead beat* dads and single mothers. Some men take care of their families without [the help of] a mother [figure] or spouse. Yet and still they get no acknowledgement or appreciation. In fact, when a woman takes on that same role, she's perceived as an angel, *Heaven sent* or just a dedicated mother. There's nothing wrong with that, but as a man he's told [by society] that *that's what's expected of you*. He doesn't get the same credit. The one day of the year [Father's day] that he's honored gets overlooked by Mother's Day.

This leaves me to examine the role that men play in society. It's true not too many of us step up to the plate, but we must always honor and appreciate those who *do* take care of their responsibility. Because of the lack of love [from so many men] for their families, women are replacing men in society and in their homes. Independent and single mothers are doing it all; realizing that they don't need a man. That may be true [from what I hear], but there's no satisfaction like the joy you feel when you [a woman] knows that she has a loving and dedicated man.

But we can't blame them, it's us [men] who need to prove that we do belong, and we will be there for our families. We need to rebuild that joy our ladies felt [at one time or another] by knowing we were there for them. We need to show society that we are dedicated and strong men. We need to teach our sons, nephews, brothers, and cousins [etc.] that a man takes care of his family. He [needs to] man up to his responsibilities. A [real] man loves his family so much [that] he will work his butt off to make sure [that] they are taken care of.

It's time men step up and realize our women shouldn't do it [family responsibilities] alone. We need to stay involved in our families like men. Men, there's no reason to run away from your responsibility .The future has many unknown certainties. But let's not worry about if we will be a part of it. Let's make the future, a future men can say they helped produce. By molding and constructing the mind of our leaders of tomorrow-which is our kids.

Without a strong leadership, our kids' future could look really dim. If we as men step up we could, and will make a difference. But we have to step up. Be willing to admit you made a mistake. Be honest enough to accept it. Be man enough to fix it. Lead by example because our kids are watching us. The time [clock of our future] is ticking [time is ticking and the time is now]. Men in society need to step up. Only a coward runs from his responsibility.

Lastly, we as men need to rebuild our role as honorable men, [and it] starts first with our family. [Let me illustrate it like this] Our family should be our *business*. Let's keep it thriving and pushing forward to ensure its success, with our spouse as an equal *business* partner. How can society function without us doing our part? Honestly, tell me what your thoughts are-am I right or wrong? Are men overlooked in society (because so many of us run from our responsibilities)?

Darrell R. Freeman Jr.,
Author of
A Dreadful Day and *Remember My Name*
Betraying My Father

Being single is only a bad place...

...If you want and allow it to be.

It's a part of your

Process before your Possession.

Contents

PREFACE

I have always had many male friends. But yet as I got older, I realized that at the age of 34 years old, I have never had a complete and successful date. It *just* dawned on me that in a little over eight years after being married (or so I thought) I have never had a *real* date. You know the date when the guy comes to my house, knocks on the door dressed nice and smelling good, carrying flowers, walk me to the car and assist me down any steps as a gesture (and not because I need it), opens the car door, and shuts it once I am inside. Then we go out to dinner and maybe a movie and return home. During our travels, he opens my car door and assists me out the car. When we return back to my house, he walks me to my front door, gives me a kiss on the cheek and leaves.

I can't remember ever being asked by a guy to go *steady,* and he gives me a *going steady ring.* While we are at it – I have had several marriage proposals beginning at the age of 16, but none like I dreamed. Maurice was my first marriage proposal, and he mailed me an engagement ring with a teddy bear, and photos of him getting down on one knee, and proposing to me. Lester proposed to me in the mall after we spent…no wasted a lot of money in a game arcade and on a $500 dog. He bought me a wedding ring set that I had picked out from a jewelry store. Hey, it was on sale! I-along with everyone else thought that Kyle was going to *pop the question*-especially since we had spent so many years together and discussed it. And not to mention that guy whom I really did marry (or so I thought) proposed to me over the phone and with no ring. Some proposals for marriage came while having sex. But none of the proposals ever contained the attributes of my dream marriage proposal. Whereas the guy surprises me by getting down on one knee and *popping the question* after a healthy and successful relationship was established. The proposal would precede a huge wedding day with…well I don't want to give it all away.

Although I have had bits and pieces of potentially successful relationships, I realize that I have been settling for a slice instead of getting the *whole relationship pie,* so I can enjoy as much as I want. Think of your favorite desert. Do you want to be able to indulge when you chose or be limited in your portions? I know that I am a good woman and I know that I have a lot of love to give. But it seems as though I love too hard when I shouldn't, and don't love the best when I should. Like I mentioned in my book *I Married Satan* I wonder how many men who were just supposed to be *seasonal* men in my life that I tried to keep around for a lifetime and how many men who could have potentially been sent by God to be a man for my lifetime- I pushed away and avoided them being able to occupy my heart. *Is that why I prefer to work so that I still avoid the stress of being at home, and being alone?*

Around the same time that I received that revelation, I worked at a job, which had all women in the office, except one male. And so while we were there working shift work, and to make the time go faster while we were there – we would have conversations that always seemed to have *I just don't understand* come up in them when it came to discussing men, and our relationships with them. So I posted some parts of the conversation's content on Facebook, to get responses and advice, but I didn't quit get the response that I was hoping to get in return. So I started just blatantly asking some of my male friends for advice in various dating situations of both my own, and my other female friends and acquaintances. Well, as some of those male friends who based on what could be deemed as a violation of the number one *Man Law* told me that inside scoop, I began to realize that a lot of what I thought and understood about men – I didn't, and that is why I have NEVER been on a complete great date, and/or had a truly successful relationship. Maybe the man who finally does grant my wish will be the one whom I'm ordained by God to marry.

Well, once I started having these conversations about men/boys/males and why they do the things that they do, say the things that they say, act the way that they act, and avoid commitments; I decided that I needed to share this information, and help my *sistahs* to be informed about what I was learning. This way we can all have an opportunity to be happy and have a successful relationship, once we all take into consideration this advice and these pointers. Then if we follow simple steps, rules and regulations, which came directly from males, maybe – just maybe we too can have one of those relationships that we dream of having and truly desire. We all have ideal mentalities of what we want and expect from a man based on our upbringings and various backgrounds, but the truth is that just as the Bible says *my people perish for lack of knowledge* (Hosea 4:6). Could this all possibly be another tactic used by the devil to try to destroy relationships between humans and the future of families? As one of my male friends Darron said, which confirms in a nutshell what I learned about the entire *game of dating* – "*we both male and female people have made the dating arena much more complicated than it needed to be.*" And how? In addition to our various backgrounds and upbringings, we have to now add to the equation past hurt and experiences-both negative and positive.

Ladies I have infatuated *man lines* and was able to get us some *good stuff.* Things that not only opened my eyes, but made me look at men in a whole new light. I now understand **WHY I AM STILL SINGLE**! But I now have the ability to make changes and adjustments in my life so that I can truly be the virtuous woman that I was designed to be. And this time –a man, who finds me and decides to make me his wife, will not just have a good thing, but a great thing in being in a relationship with me.

Men please understand that I only mention those who shared information with me by their first name, considering that there is a good chance that there are multiple men in and around the world with the same first name…so you cannot revoke their *man cards*. Oh that was not given to me I discovered it on one of the *Man Law* pages.

With that being said…let's get ready to decode this *Secret Fraternal Order* and the *Bitter Sweets of Man Law* to answer *Oh is that Why I'm Still Single?*

Prologue

After I finally found the strength to leave the man whom I thought that I was married to, I relocated to a city which was far enough from he and my problems, but still close enough to my family in case of an emergency. Not only did I feel that I had to escape the abusive marriage that I was in, I had to also cut the umbilical cord from my mother and grow up and start making decisions for myself. Not because I stopped loving her, but I had to begin to live and experience life as an individual and start over. Despite her always being there to support me (even today), I had to learn how to stand on my own two feet and establish my independence.

Even before I moved to Baltimore I stood out like a sore thumb. But it worsened after the move, because it was obvious that I was from some place different. I met a lot people-whether successful or not, and I quickly learned that standing on my own two feet could be very painful, and extremely hard at times. Meaning that being away from my family and friends was very hard as I was uprooted and replanted in this strange place.

One major challenge was that because I didn't know how to date…dating was kah-ray-zee. Before long I realized that I needed to chill out on the dating scene, get my life right with God and get FOCUSED. However, eight years after moving to Baltimore, and five years after having my marriage is over and a few years after God got my life back on track…I'm still single. Coming home to an empty house; cooking dinner for one and watching TV and/or writing until I fall asleep…And yet with all that is going on around me whether successful or not I still have to ask myself the question…***Why am I still single?*** I can't ask my girlfriends because many of them are either *relationship challenged* or happily married.

Yet, I fall somewhere in between…

So I went to those who could provide good insight-MEN. My conversations have now become a blueprint for conversations for whoever needs to have these conversations like book clubs; spouses; organizations; social clubs; and strangers.

Oh and in case you are wondering about the chapter numbers-this book is a continuation of my life which is documented in my first book entitled *I Married Satan.*

X.

Divine Order, Law:

Men Are Slow

Chapter 1
Men are Just Plain Slow

Before I went over this guy named George's house for the first time, I laid down the rules and told him that he had to sleep on the floor (yes at his house) and that he wasn't getting *any coochie.* Well, after us spending time watching movies and talking, it was time for bed. When I said that I was going to bed, he made sure that I was in the room comfortable and inundated with music, pillows, etc. I had on nice lingerie and made sure that I *forgot something in the living room* so that he could come and see all that I had willing and waiting for him. But to my surprise, instead of him responding how I anticipated, which was by him coming to lay down beside me on the bed, he then pulled out a blanket and pillow, and went to lie on the living room floor. *Was he really playing hard to get? I love challenges!* His lack of interest made me want to be intimate with him even more. I called him into the room and asked him to give me a good night hug. Then *oops* I accidently fell on the bed and he ended up on top of me. He still didn't respond like I wanted him too. He got up and went back in to the living room to resume his position on the floor. I then invited him back to *his* room. Then I told him that he could sleep head to foot in the bed. I guess he finally got the hint because his response was a lot better this time.

He said, *"I sleep naked"*.

Although I wanted to say *"Duh, that's the point"*, I said, *"That's fine"*.

Then he lay in the bed beside me and did not touch me. I had to scoot over closer and closer to him almost knocking him off the bed before my attempts finally encouraged him to *hold me*…This is one of the reasons that I say men are just plain slow! He made me work extremely hard…no pun intended.

Although we as women are similar to one another, each one of us has our own "twist". Therefore, we cannot expect a man to *just know* what we are thinking, how we think things through, why we are thinking this way, and where this thinking is coming from, but most of all-how he is supposed to act and/or react to our thoughts and actions. We have to give a man time to learn and catch our hints. Typically, if he's been hurt before, he will tend to be more cautious when allowing himself to engage in new relationships. In other words, if you say *no you aint getting any tonight* but don't actually mean it – he may actually accept that, and not try. Contrary to what we believe, there are still some gentlemen in the world. If a man actually adheres to our hints, sometimes we feel let down or disappointed and believe that that is all he wanted. But if he tends to ignore our hints and secretly decoded messages we feel neglected and/or challenged. A good challenge can either be fun or detrimental. However, a woman is supposed to be a challenge – not the man. Whether you chose to be the challenge or the challenger, remember that reverse psychology can back fire and deprive you.

For all of you women who are looking for the prefect guy, there is no department store of man parts and personalities. I know…I know you are probably thinking that there are adult novelty *toy stores,* but I'm speaking in terms of live human being body part variety stores. We can't just go into a store and place our order for the type of man that we want based on catalog offerings. It would be nice, but the only thing that we can do is make our request and petitions to God, and pray that our request line up with His will for the mate that He (God) designed us for. Notice I said *"the mate that God designed **us for**"* not the *"mate God designed for **us**."* That is because in Genesis God put Adam to sleep opened his body took out Adam's rib (Genesis 2: 18-25) and made Eve – his wife. She was created **<u>FROM</u>** and designed **<u>FOR</u>** Adam not Adam **<u>FOR</u>** Eve. For those of you who don't know the story, the reason that Eve was made from Adam's rib is because every other one of God's creations had suitable mates and

Adam was not attracted to any of them and could not see himself mating with them and the Lord God said, *"It is not good for the man to be alone. I will make a helper suitable for him."* (Genesis 2:18). So God made something – no someone special for Adam. Ladies you were made and created and designed for a man too!

If you pick your mate yourself instead of allowing him to find or meet you, then your selection may only last for a short while because after the looks wear off and you are no longer attracted to him, your relationship may end. You know when his muscles turn to fat; his six pack turns to a keg; his nice hair cut is no longer needed because he is bald etc. (Side Note: However, if you allow yourself to be found by a man who is pursuing after God's will for his life, and striving to live a life which pleases God, your relationship may be smoother and more lucrative. Here's how and why: a man who is trying to live a "Godly life" is more likely to apply Godly principles to his own personal life. He will then also try to implement Godly principles and values in to the relationship and watch this – your life. He may not be the "perfect" (the bible says in Job 1:8 *that there is but one perfect man who ever walked the earth and that was Jesus Christ*) 100% saint type but as you try to practice God's values and principles, and he tries you can both encourage one another because iron sharpens iron (*Iron sharpeneth iron; so a man sharpeneth the countenance of his friend* Proverbs 27: 17).

Chapter 2
How to Really Get
What You Want From a Man

I once dated a guy who when I told him my expectations and desires, he tried to accommodate (ok there was actually more than one in my life time but for the purpose of this chapter let's focus on this one). For instance, I told him that I never expected to open a door for myself – and soon after whenever we went out, he made a conscious decision to unlock my car door first and open doors when we entered or exited buildings. I really thought that he had potential as a great mate. That is until I found out that he was really doing things to keep me content so that there would be the illusion that he was really into me. I started feeling that he was seeing someone else and that I had transitioned from being the *only* to the *main* one. Even though I saw him just about every day – It was like I was the only one giving anything in the relationship, and that he was the only one always reaping all of the benefits. I went from feeling wanted and special to feeling as though I was *just there*. I went from being able to *pop up* at his house (and he mine) to one day while I was riding over to his house with a mechanic to fix his truck I saw him leaving with another girl in his vehicle. He pretended as though he didn't see me. The mechanic who was also a male gave me the "maybe he didn't know it was you because you were in a different vehicle excuse." About an hour later the guy who I was trying to help to get his truck fixed called me and when I asked him about the "drive by" he denied that it happened and said that it was his next door neighbor. It made absolutely no sense since he was such a private person (or that he made me to believe he was), and did not interact with too many people outside of his immediate circle of family and friends. After some time we talked, I forgave him, and he continued to implement my request for him to be a gentleman. Even though he and I didn't work out in a relationship, we still remain friends. Plus, as a bonus to our friendship, I have the bragging rights of depositing and encouraging the gentleman tactics that he learned with me to his next relationship.

The example discussed above is vague and general has a principle to it which works like this: to really get what you want from a man is a simple yet complex task for women to do. Simply ask him. A man will hear what you say, and if he really likes and/or cares about you he will listen and accommodate. However, if he is just going through the motions of being with you, or only with you to obtain certain *benefits – like sex, money, food, clothes, gas for his vehicle, minutes for his cell phone, bills paid, haircuts, shoes, a babysitter for kids etc.*, then he may only do enough to keep you content. Why are you settling? This applies to both physical and emotional things that we want and request from our male mates.

So LaDonna, is there a certain way I should ask him? LaDonna says: *I'm glad you asked.*

Ready ladies…here is the simple process:

Step 1:	Politely ask him for what you want and/or would like for him to do.
Step 2:	Wait and give him time to do it in *HIS* time.
Step 3:	If he still has not done the task in your time-repeat step 1 and 2
Step 4:	Finally, give him one reminder because he may have honestly forgotten.

Notice that I said **ONE** reminder. Just one reminder of your request-*Why?* Men cannot stand to be nagged and they have a tendency to rebel if we nag them too many times for something. (*Better to live on a corner of the roof than share a house with a quarrelsome wife.* Proverbs 21:9) Let's say that you would like for your mate to take out the trash. Now wait before we go any further, the first thing to consider is that if you two are not living together you cannot require him to take out YOUR trash-the trash that you created. He may offer to do so (if he is being nice) but it is not his job. No one is obligated to take out your trash or maintain your household but you. Didn't you tell someone *this is my house and I pay all the bills*? I would sound foolish to some of you if I said even in this economy you should not be shacking up (living with a man if you are unmarried). But it's the truth. If you live together and are married, it is assumed that you two have had conversations while dating about what is and is not expected and/or required of both of you in the relationship between you and your life long mate. So, if you and he are living together, then you should have sat down before signing the lease, mortgage papers and marriage license, and discussed your roles within the household.

Hopefully you two did not rush into moving in with one another for ulterior motives like financial benefits or because you needed a place to live and had little to no other options. If any of the above is true a conversation needs to be had ASAP between you and your mate and be prepared because some changes and decisions may have to be made immediately. Like what? I'm not in your household so I can't answer that. But be strategic, realistic, open, honest and proactive. However if it is too late and all hell is breaking lose it is time to go!

XI.

Imperfection, Disorder, Incompleteness:

Stop Messing Up Good Men

Chapter 3
...Because You Are a Bad Woman

From what I hear, it is rumoured that women mentally mature earlier, and more quickly than men. However, there has recently become a fad for cougars. Not the cute cats that some of us wish we could own as pets; but older women dating younger men.

We all may have had to deal with males who are more focused on themselves, their careers and getting established, than on the women in their lives. And that's cool. I think it is an awesome venture for a man to have his life on a successful track, before getting into a relationship. I imagine that being with a man who is emotionally; and spiritually; <u>AND</u> financially stable is a wonderful and reassuring feeling. However it may be hard for a man to rest assured in those same feelings of confidence of being with a "stable" female because it may appear that so many women have been *damaged* emotionally and mentally recently. These same *damaged* women, especially if the woman is older than the man with whom she is dating; tend to mess up good men.

Older women who date younger men seem to transfer their emotional issues onto younger men who appear to have potential. How, because they are taught to be more mature and have accomplishments like having a job and/or money; their own car; their own place etc. But mentally because of her past hurts and disappointments of previous relationships, especially is she was married before she transfers her hurt and pain to the male mentally, emotionally and spiritually. She may act and speak accusations; display her insecurities; lash out and more. Her current male spouse may be completely loyal and faithful, but she ultimately damages him because of her issues. Conversely, some women have become so desperate that they would even settle for just a male wanting her. But what happens is that sometimes the younger male is damaged because he too has a desire to be wanted and loved, but older women have taken him on an emotional roller coaster causing him to have emotional, trust and affection issues. Being with an older woman gives that male *bragging rights* to his male friends about being with an older woman. (Side note: His friends may even encourage him to pursue the relationship with an older woman as well, but be careful because the same male friends who encourage him to continue the relationship may also be the same ones who get jealous later).

When an older woman deals with a younger man who is mentally less mature, she may confuse him. When she deals with one who's more mature than she (even if she does not admit it) and *ready* for a relationship it causes her to do introspection mentally because he then too keeps her *on her toes* and they both enjoy their relationship.

I dated a few guys who were younger in age than me. The problem was that they expressed an interest in me and I had that desire to be desired. I did not require my newly established requirements, but instead I was *easy*, allowing shortcuts. This caused them to make attempts to spend more time with me, but for me the thrill of the moment had passed. There was no longer a need inside of me to have them want me so they superficially served their temporary purpose of filling space in my life with no strings, and no commitments. And yet I still was single and alone.

Once we emotionally screw up a man we mess him up for the next woman who may be compatible with him, and a suitable mate for him. But because he has been taught to have trust issues and his heart has been hurt, the new and potential female's successful relationship is compromised. She has already lost before she began and now has to put forth an extra effort to reassure this man that she is not the same as the previous women he has dealt with and that things would be done differently if he were in a relationship with her. Also that her kind gestures that she is showing toward him are sincere and genuine and that she sees that he is a great guy with great potential. But he may have lost confidence in himself and love. It has become easier for him to guard his heart than to have to cope with the potential of another prospective heartbreak. Then once he has been hurt, the next woman that he has dealings with would be hurt and the dominoes effect begins. This leads to messy, ugly and potentially devastating breakups.

We as women tend to be vindictive and spiteful to do whatever we can to inflict pain, hurt and potentially emotional and sometimes physical and permanent scars on males. He probably too is in a mental tug of war between what his *boys* are telling him, what his heart feels, and what his mind is computing that his eyes see. *Oh*, and it could only worsen if we infuse a court ordered judgment of child support.

Child Support is a Hustle is one of the most thought provoking slogans on a t-shirt that I've seen recently. When I first saw this shirt, it was being worn by one of my fellow train riders Marcel, and it sparked a conversation. From what I knew about him he was a decent guy who worked but also had to pay child support. His child's mother, like a lot of woman recently, have come to see child support payments as being fashionable as they take decent and not just *dead beat* dads to court no matter how damaging the mandatory payments can be to the lives of those men.

I met a guy named Darrell once who had a fairly decent job as an apartment complex maintenance man. He had three children by two different women. (Side note: I tend to be turned off by a man who has "a bunch" of kids. Especially if the *multiple kids*, are with multiple women. Like when I met this one guy who just said that he had two kids and over time during conversations, I discovered that he had at least ten which he admitted to. His favourite thing to tell me was "*so what if I can take care of them*". To me if a man does have multiple kids by multiple women, that is telling me a few different things: (1) he is having sex unprotected which can put my body in danger of catching an STD and/or AIDS; (2) he is irresponsible (3) he may not be able to commit; and (4) he may just want to get me pregnant and I may be left being a single mom. Besides him having many kids means cutting into our finances if we get married. I'm not being selfish-it's just a preference that I have. Also, men please be honest about the number of kids that you have up front and at the beginning stages of a relationship. Give the woman you are considering creating and maintaining a relationship with the benefit of the doubt to decide if she wants to deal with you and all your babies. It is better to tell her up front than to let her find out later. If you do tell her up front she may be willing to continue the relationship but if you wait she may be more likely to leave you than to stay. Generally, you may think that the more of her time and heart that she has invested in to yall's relationship, the more she will want to stay and make it work with you.

However, from my stand point, it is always better to tell me **ANYTHING** and **EVERYTHING** up front and then let me decide if I am going to deal with it, and you, than for you to make my decision for me. If I find out later that a man wasn't up front and honest especially about the number of kids that he has, then my trust diminishes and can no longer be established with and for him. How can it? If he can lie about his own seed(s), he may be able to lie to me about anything).

Anyway, back to the story. Despite him being incarcerated off and on for ten years of his life, he was attempting to make the best out of the years he had left in life and of his freedom, which he vowed to maintain. To make a long story short at the age of thirty nine years old, he was finally making some lead way and recreating and establishing his life on a great track to become very successful. Well because of back child support payments being owed and delinquent, his driver's license was suspended. Then just as he thought that he was beginning to move his life forward and because of the deductions being made from his pay check for the payments, he could barely afford his monthly expenses like rent; gas and electric payments; food; etc. *Was child support absolutely necessary? Did the mothers have to take such extreme measures for payments? Didn't he just get out of jail and is trying to get established? Should he be given some time to make an attempt on catching up on payments?* Now I know that there are two sides to every story and he could be leaving out some points of the one that he is telling me, but I personally don't believe in taking a man to child support court to support his child/children unless absolutely necessary. However, both of his children's' mothers did not have a problem doing so.

This scenario is common amongst a couple of different male friends that I have come across, causing the males to be hurt emotionally and financially and to barely be able to keep *their head above water* in either case. Do they really have to spend the rest of their lives barely surviving so that the mother of their child/children lives happily ever after until her last payment? Let's be honest ladies the kids often times get the leftovers of the payments. I've seen a lot of mothers wearing nice clothes; have their hair done, and more and yet the kids look a *hot mess.* Their hair looks uncombed/uncut; their clothes are raggedy; and despite the mothers looking good – and again the children look a *hot mess!*

It appears that despite some males trying to support their children with love and emotional support – child support payments act as a way to revenge him for not being in a relationship with the child/children's mother(s). *If he isn't going to be one big happy family with me then I'll get him back; he is going to feel the emotional pain that I feel financially.* Do some females think that they can purchase peace or revenge? Again, causing a domino effect for future relationships.

Systematically the legal system has sided with females. There are also times when women have gotten men arrested, falsely accused, in trouble with the legal system, their driver's license revoked; terminated from their employment, and/or evicted from their residence, caused distension between his family; and may have gotten the male beat up verbally, physically, mentally and emotionally, and so much more. Females if it proven that you two are not supposed to be together in a relationship, be woman enough to walk away, please do not use child support to try and buy revenge only financially.

Remember karma is real and the Bible does say *that you reap what you sow (*Galatians 6:7)…think back to the damage that you've done to males…ever wonder why all hell may be breaking out in your life, and why bad things keep burying you? It's never too late to apologize, even if you feel that a man is not in his role as a father.

It's no one's fault that men are not in their roles as fathers to their kids. Some women are not allowing men to be men and are trying to be overly nurturing to their men. For many years many woman have had to be in their roles as mommy and attempt to play daddy in kids' lives. But is it fair to blame the other parent when both parents are absent from their assigned and assumed role?

Some people blame men who are away due to incarceration. Now I have learned from having conversations with a few guys I have met or know like Darnell who are current or former inmates the crime that they are *in* jail for was for validation of themselves and for their children. For example, they sold drugs to make money or they pulled the gun to protect themselves and/or their families. Some of the men I know personally had given up hope and faith that they could get a job, and so they did what they knew and what was learned from their fathers/daddies/role models…being on and working "the block". And in an effort to be in our rightful place, we have to not keep them away from their father, unless there are safety issues-JUST DON'T! Remember you chose him or let him choose you.

Maturity plays a huge role in a man being responsible. A person who knows of better will do better. (Side note: if he hasn't had any role models then he is going to make a lot of what we deem and decide are mistakes, because he didn't have any examples or lessons on being the type of man that he should be). At least give a man the opportunity to try. From what I hear parenting does not come with a manual. If you have a man who is willing to be a father to his child/children let him try. We sometimes attract males who resemble our father whether he was active or not in our life. This doesn't necessarily mean that you have truly attracted and/or had a baby by a *deadbeat* or that your *baby's daddy* should be punished or rewarded because of your father's actions. And please do not pronounce the curses of the type of man that your mother or you have chosen to reproduce with on to your children.

Women have a tendency to transfer their issues to their daughters, and your mother, grandmother, aunt, stepmother (or whomever may have raised you) may have done just that – transferred some *issues* and ideology about men to you. Am I the only one who has ever said "*I'm turning into my mother*"? Or have you been told that you act just like your grandmother or grandfather? (On a side note: My grandmother always said "*don't take no mess from anyone*" and my grandfather said "*use common sense*". So I am a combination of both.)

Your bitterness and hate may have caused you to live in your own tomb or dead place, where you are mad, sad and alone. When you allow seeds of hurt, bitterness etc. to establish root in your heart, the harvest is going to be hurt and pain until you find deliverance through God, much like a man named Legion in the bible. *And they came over unto the other side of the sea, into the country of the Gadarenes. And when he was come out of the ship, immediately there met him out of the tombs a man with an unclean spirit, Who had his dwelling among the tombs; and no man could bind him, no, not with chains: Because that he had been often bound with fetters and chains, and the chains had been plucked asunder by him, and the fetters broken in pieces: neither could any man tame him. And always, night and day, he was in the mountains, and in the tombs, crying, and cutting himself with stones. But when he saw Jesus afar off, he ran and worshipped him, And cried with a loud voice, and said, "What have I to do with thee, Jesus, thou Son of the most high God? I adjure thee by God, that thou torment me not"*. (Mark 5:1-7). If you talk about hurt, pain and failures etc. long enough then that is what you will become and you could possibly sow those same seeds in to your children. Even when you are no longer in a relationship that you were not happy in-it's as if you have cut off the fruit which came from the harvest of those bad seeds but you never uprooted the bad issues. This is why it is very important that you pray for and get deliverance from God for the uprooting and destruction of those bad issues. Then get attached to a Bible based, word teaching, Holy Spirit filled church; and not one who just has good music and good fellowship, events or appearances by a lot of celebrities. Make sure that you will be able to grow in the word, teachings, and knowledge of God, as your relationship of and faith in Him increases. Oh and by the way it is important that above anything else you forgive, because strife hinders prayers.

The bottom line is that men who are responsible will be in their children's lives but those who aren't - may not. The first way to avoid the headache and heartache is to practice abstinence but if you *must have it*, please use some form of birth control. That way you won't have any added mistakes (*e.g. STDs*) or blessings (*e.g. babies*). Men if you aren't ready to be tied to this woman for a lifetime, then the same as mentioned above, definitely applies to you. Despite advances in science, it definitely takes two people to have unprotected sex and reproduce, Oh, if your family is dysfunctional and a lot of babies are being born out of wedlock (the parents not being married to one another when the baby is conceived), please break the cycle of life that you have been taught and wait.

Kids do what they are taught and often imitate what they see. If they are taught racism-then they are going to be racist. If they are spoiled and undisciplined-then they are going to grow up being spoiled, undisciplined and thinking that they own the world. If they see a woman being abused by a man-then they are going to grow up thinking that they are either supposed to be abusers or that it is ok to be abused. With that being said, they also learn how to interact with another individual within a relationship. However, if they see a woman frequently with different men then how or when does a child learn how to have a successful relationship with or without both of their parents being together in a relationship?

When you have kids and decide that you want to date someone other than that child/those children's other parent, there can be a grey area. On one hand you have to listen to your kids but don't let your kids set the boundaries for your relationship or dictate to you who you can and cannot date. Listen to their input but they may be resenting your potential spouse and/or jealous. Or they may like the person because the person spoils them with materialist items and with a false sense of temporary parental structure. Ultimately you are still the parent and your kids need to respect your decision. Kids tend to imitate what they see. If they see you behaving some kind of way when dealing with members of the opposite sex your children may behave the same way. This is why we hear so many warnings about not allowing our kids to witness us being in relationships which have domestic violence in them. (Side note: Whether you are close to your parent and they are single, your single parents should not be allowed to jeopardize your relationship because they are afraid to be alone or abandoned because you have a relationship and they don't).

Anyway, you will still have to balance and prioritize the relationship that you have with your kids and the relationship that you have with your potential spouse. Since I personally don't have children of my own, I can't say that it is easy or hard. But I can say that the balance of the two relationships is important and intricate to the success of either and both-the relationship with your children and/or potential spouse. You don't want either to feel neglected or less important or ignored. Also, you don't want to have either failed because of unnecessary drama; issues, and avoidable situations. Now as far as the needs of each party/member of the individual relationships, they are for you to identify and tend to them. That may be a lot for you to remember so you will have to get in to the practice until they become habitual. But it shouldn't be stressful. The relationship with your potential mate should eventually parallel the relationship with your *babies*, and eventually, it should *flow* naturally if the relationships are meant to be.

In any type of relationship (business, pleasure, with his friends etc.) that your man is involved with, if you want to see different or better from him, have him spend time with different-or better. In other words if you want marriage-have him spend time with married men; wealth-have him spend time around men who work hard and are financially stable; to have good hygiene-have him spend time with "pretty boys" etc. Hopefully you get my point.

Chapter 4
Get Out Your Feelings

I am really feelin' this guy – he seems to be like a breath of fresh air from typical guys that I have been dating lately. He seems to be doing ever-ree-thang right and it seems that he is really sharing mutual feelings with me. However, despite my feelings, the Bible says *that he that findeth a wife findeth a good thing, and obtainith favor of the Lord (Proverbs 18:22)*…so let a man decide that he wants you and let him realize that he wants to be with you and he will work hard to keep you. In other words, let him chose you as his lady and get out your feelings.

This has to be one of the most contrasting statements for a woman to hear since women are emotional creatures. It's hard…Lord knows – I know it's hard. I am one of those people who fall in love very easy and quickly. I tend to cling on to the guy who expresses interest, and who can catch and keep my interest and attention.

There was a guy who I worked with named Devon (I know in general you're not supposed to date someone you work with or who lives close by your home because of the drama that could unfold), who seemed cool. We met on a whim. I was drinking a soda in the company's break room and our eyes made contact and seemed to lock in on each other. I thought to myself *dang why do you keep staring at me-speak already.* Well, me being me I took the imitative and said *"how you doing"*.

"How you doing", he respond. *"No… I'm not thirsty"*.

"*You can have some*", I replied with hidden flirtatious insinuations, as I held out my cup in a gesture to invite his advances. He walked off and I went on my way.

Then on another day on my way in to work I noticed him as I was getting out of my car and I once again was carrying a beverage, and he returned the antics by saying "*I'm thirsty*". As I continued once again to walk into the building, I smiled and gestured as if I was handing him the cup again and said "*you can have some*".

We flirted at work a few MORE times, and I had to sometimes contain myself. Later that month we had a discussion about me purchasing him a soda. That was another ice breaker for us to converse. I hadn't been close enough to him to see what he really looked like and I didn't know until his co-worker described him as *the guy who also lived in BMORE*. To me that meant a potential co-car pooler, because it was at least a forty-five minute drive from my house to my job. Upon closer observation, he wasn't that bad looking at all either. He was light skinned and had green eyes. Now I typically am not attracted to light skin, pretty eyed men, but it was nice to feel pursued by this one.

One day during my lunch break I was in the Break Room (yes again) working on the *I Married Satan* stage play, and he walked in, but our conversation was very short. If I remember correctly, I think other people were either in the room or had entered the room shortly after him. Days later, I thought about him and felt drawn to and curious about him because he wasn't aggressive or forthcoming. The carpooling thing was the perfect reason to communicate with him and I had already planned that the next time that I saw him, I would converse more with him about that and whatever else that I could. I was ready! But he didn't come in there that day. Later that day, I walked into the area of the job where he worked and asked him about him living in Baltimore. He was working and once again our brief conversation had an audience of other co-workers, so I was careful to keep things professional and very vague, so that they would not suspect anything outside of the conversation that we were having about carpooling. Nope they weren't going to be able to accuse me of fraternizing. He obviously had become intrigued with me as well and soon our *"running into each others"* became a daily meeting with him in the break room as he came and joined me for lunch on his own, and we talked more. Day by day the conversation was becoming very intriguing, and one day he asked me for a hug. That hug made me *melt* as a woman.

I began to look forward to seeing and hugging him every day. Soon after I gave him my phone number and address, and the text messages started occurring. We started making plans to hang out together outside of work and my feelings were starting to really develop, based on his promises. However, I quickly began to snap out of them because of the repetitive and habitual disappointments of feeling like he stood me up. *Me?* Then I stopped trusting in him. *Did he have a girlfriend already? Did he work another job? Why was it ok for him to get my hopes up and then so easily let me down?* Okay after he kept disappointing me over and over again his actions asked and caused for and earned vengeance. Enough was enough! There had to be consequences for him playing around with my feelings and emotions, and It wasn't until after the fourth time of his excuse filled explanation episodes that I thanked him. He didn't know that I was thanking him because his *stand ups* preserved my celibacy track record. Originally I had planned that he would find out until this book was released, but he again came in to the lunch break room and I just happen to have finished this chapter. So he read it and now knows. Had I become a *game piece* to him? *Or was he catching feelings for me even though he had a girlfriend somewhere?* Anyway, he still made several mentions of us *hanging out* but I got stood up way more than expected, and began to lose faith even when he assured me that "us" would happen.

Then one day he came and knocked on the door to my home but I didn't answer because I didn't hear it. He left a book of matches on my car's window. I thought that either the wind blew it on my car's window, or that one of my neighbours was being trifling, I didn't know that it was his *calling card,* so I threw them on the ground. He called the next morning to let me know that it was he who had placed the matches on my car. Was he trying to string me along? Or was this still part of his *shenanigans*? I wanted to know, so I gave him the opportunity to explain.

He explained that his job as a truck driver had a crazy schedule and although he had every intention of making good on his request to spend time with me, sometimes his schedule got in the way. I understood more now that I saw and comprehended clearly and without feelings being involved. You did notice that I didn't say that I believed him but merely entertained him. And now it seemed like the more that I ignored him, the more he made a conscious decision to call and text and/or stop by. Until… he no longer worked at the job.

He texted me one day and I was extremely busy at work. I couldn't sit there and text him continuously and one of my text responded *"what's up/what do you need?"* He responded with a few texts after my response, but one in particular *jumped out there* at me.

"I was just saying hye" [yes spelled like that] *you aint all that."*

I didn't respond. But I thought about it *if I'm not all that then why are you sending me so many texts? Why are you even taking time out of your life to contact me at all?*

A few weeks later I was having dinner with my mother for my birthday and he started calling from two separate cell phones. He left messages and called consecutively. When I didn't answer he called back. Hmmm…sounds like someone who DEFINITELY is not all that lol.

The playing field had changed once he decided that his feelings were real towards me, and that he did in fact want me. However, by the time he made a choice to want me, I was already done with any thought or feelings for him. He called me a few times after but the conversation went from friendly conversation to disrespectful and sexual inquiries. I began thinking with my mind, and ignored the lust-fullness of my body, and I was able to stand firm and say *NO*! No I was no longer seeing him through my emotional vision and therefore I was able to maintain boundaries.

Once we are able to see the truths of a man's intentions as well as how is really treating us, we are able to have peace. But how are you supposed to do that? Get out your feelings. This means that your mind has to be the part of your body which interprets his communication towards you. Not your heart or what's between your legs. There will be time to involve your feelings later. Falling head over heels can cause you to fall flat on your face. Oh and by the way, selling drugs also took up a lot of his time and energy. And now I see that once again God was protecting me.

Chapter 5
Cheese Steak Love

Have you ever ordered a cheese steak (or your favourite sandwich) from your local carryout restaurant or favourite corner store? If you are like me, when you get it the outer aluminium foil may be crinkled; the white sandwich… wrapping paper may be tearing and wrinkled; the paper bag it all comes in is greasy, and on the verge of breaking. Meat and toppings are starting to fall all over the place because there is so much of it jammed packed into that sandwich. It just smells so good.

Personally, I like to watch my sandwich being prepared as the meat is dropped on the grill with the seasonings, onions and cheese all concocted to create this masterpiece. It contains tons of calories. So despite my heart's desire to indulge in it, I limit my appointments with my *"dream sandwich"* to occasional times. I know that too much is definitely not good for me. But once I unwrap this sandwich and take the first bite…*I'm in love*! Forget what it looks like or how messy it is or how many calories that it has or the fact that they aren't good for me. I'm about to tear this sandwich up! It may not look the best or be the most appealing but the process before the possession is forgotten as I indulge. (*Side note: this chapter just reminded me that I need to take a road trip to Philly to get a cheesesteak from Max's or Gino's-my bad, a sistah gets hungry with all this writing lol*)

Much like an ideal mate once I get pass the outer wrapping of what he may look like appearance wise on the outside, which may or may not be my desired preference, I am truly satisfied. A man with a great heart can come in any type of *outer wrapping*. He may not be sexy or attractive according to everyone else's' standards. But get pass the outer and see his heart. Does he respect you? Does he genuinely love you? Does he treat your kids well? Maybe he spent more time making sure that the *inner he* was clean, neat and attractive. I personally would prefer to have a man who is spiritually clean, neat and attractive combined with being attractive on the outside. And inner beauty would definitely trump his outer if I had to choose. Besides there may come a time when you can make suggestions without imposing or trying to change him totally; Just a reminder to make suggestions and not demands.

I remember being told a story as a little girl by my Great Aunt Martha whom a lot if not all of the family called Girlfriend, about two girls. One was beautiful on the outside but even animals would stay away from her because they could sense the ugliness of her inner being personally and spiritually. There was another girl who had less favourable looks on the outside. But animals flocked to her because they could sense the gentle and kind spirit about her. The moral of the fable is that it is more important to have inner beauty than to have outer beauty-even to animals. You have to make sure that your inner beauty also matches your outer beauty. This is how and why you may have seen the most unlikely matched (in our opinion) couples as far as looks are concerned. You know the really short guy with the really tall girl; the really heavy set guy with the girl with the awesome body and appearance etc. It is because they are in a relationship with each other's heart and possibly in their minds they are the most attractive individuals for each other…we can't judge or read their thoughts…

Don't dwell on a man's looks and base your feelings and relationship on it. But instead build your relationship on what is in each other's minds first then hearts. The outer looks should be a bonus to your attraction to his relationship with God, his mind, and his loving heart. Don't miss your opportunity with a man just because his appearance doesn't match your ideal mate. Maybe your ideas of whom your ideal mate is keeping you single.

Chapter 6
Mamaz Boys

I met a guy named George who told me that he felt that his mother was very verbally abusive to him. Therefore he made up in his mind, that once he had tried to do everything that he could to make his relationship with her mother work (and it still didn't), that he was no longer going to be habitually hurt by her and that they were no longer going to be in contact or have a relationship. He said that she used to talk about how unsuccessful she felt that he was and made comments about him trying to be someone's father and he could barely take care of himself, and more.

God has blessed him with two daughters of his own. He decided in his mind that he was not going to treat his daughters (and any other subsequent women in his life), like his mother treated him. When he and I went out he was very respectful to me, and I thought that he was the only child and a *mama's boy*. I had no idea that he was the opposite.

We shared many conversations and one in particular resounds in my memory. It started out as us typically getting to know each other from conversation. Whenever I go out with a guy who shows interest, I almost always pick up on how far the friendship will go based on long-term goals. I want to get married and have kids. This particular guy may want to get married but doesn't want any more kids. We also shared many dreams, goals, and decisions. But throughout the duration of our conversations, I had to come to a point where I had to be blunt and honest; especially when he told me more of his story, which included him having a vasectomy. After our conversation, I shared with him that I felt that him having a vasectomy was unfair to the woman whom he may one day marry, because it seems that he only did it to *cut off* the pain that the women he truly loved including his two daughters' mothers have caused him. I further explained to him that I believe a child is a gift handed down from God to parents (*Lo, children are an heritage of the LORD: and the fruit of the womb is his reward.* Psalms 127:3). A baby is also the ultimate expression of love from a woman to a man, since a woman's entire body is taken over by that child and that child's needs once she is pregnant. I had already decided that he and I could only be friends because of his vasectomy and other issues later discovered. My male friend seems to have conditioned his mind to block out the hurt and pain in his heart. To avoid the possibility of having to go through more hurt and pain; and to avoid the possibility and risk of having any more children; he *snipped it.* He may or may not realize it but the hurt and pain could still happen in his mind and heart not just because of what is or is not functioning between his legs. Maybe in his mind the hurt, pain and cost of loving someone and then being hurt by them is minimized, but the reality of the situation is that the possibility is still there. It's up to him to prepare himself and accept that <u>all</u> relationships have ups and downs. Personally, I would be afraid of a *too perfect* relationship, meaning that it has no issues.

A man's relationship with his momma may not dictate how he treats you. She may have been *messed up*/severely damaged mentally, physically, emotionally and spiritually like the women we discussed in Chapter 3. However, because of her behavior and how she treated him, a man may treat you better than he treats his momma. Not because he loves her less, but because they don't have a relationship. Deep down he wants that relationship with her, but they haven't found a common denominator to build on or figured out how to have a loving and successful relationship. Although a relationship with his mama is what he wants and what we he may make observations off of as a basis as to how he is going to treat us, his relationship with God is what matters.

Now let's take a moment to talk about *Mamaz Boys.* It's time to go and leave a relationship with a man when his relationship has crossed the line from loving, taking care of and respecting his momma, to her being in every aspect of your relationship. Now, please note that if you two are only dating and not married, his mother or daughter(s) may be a priority in his life over you. It is only when you become his wife that the order of priority shifts. He is his mother's son not her spouse. Now I'm not saying that you should get mad when he does things for her. The Bible tells us to *honor our father and mother so that our days will be long on the earth.* (Exodus 20:12). But it also says: *therefore shall a man **leave his father** and his **mother**, and shall **cleave** unto **his wife**: and they shall be one flesh* (Genesis 2:24). Only a Mamaz Boy will avoid the change in relationship status between him and his mother; to him and his spouse.

A Mamaz Boy example: stereotypically a mother's son is the child in which she bonds with different and more closely than her daughter. I don't know how or why it just seems to happen. She may be harder on her daughter while she is raising her, but because she has a soft spot in her heart for her son, she tends to be more lenient and affectionate.

I had a guy I was dating once and his mother had him when she was 33 years old. When he and I were together at their house especially, we could not have a moment alone to ourselves. Yes, he still lived at home with his parents at 34 years old, and was the only child. I never did figure out if their relationship was close because of the guilt she felt from spending time on drugs and was consistently trying to reconcile their relationship and make up for lost time. The thing is, as long as she forgave herself; asked God for forgiveness and repented she was already forgiven and free from the guilt. Obviously, he wasn't still condemning her because he loved spending time with his mom. Wait…it's not totally wrong for him to still be at home, he had less individual bills but at the cost of independence. She would ask him to look for things like her shoes etc. under her bed for her while she was dressed in just a slip. And he felt comfortable enough to walk around the house in a t-shirt and a pair of *tighty whiteys* because *she had seen him before.* Now, there is a difference between seeing your son as a baby and *SEEING* him as a grown man. She didn't want him to move out and get his own place; but instead at over 60 years old she decided that she wanted to move out of the completely paid for house-a house that she and her husband together with their son lived; and purchase a new house. Wait, there is more! Her son was going to help pay the mortgage. Sounds like a *good son* right? Well when I needed a place to live, she finally allowed me to stay in the house with them. The guy and I decided that the basement of the house would be our *little abode* despite her insisting that he and I move to the top floor above her room in two separate rooms. This meant no privacy, even though he and I had discussed marriage, I didn't have a ring on my finger. Also, now that I think about it, I'm not sure if she was trying to get us to sleep in separate rooms to omit our privacy or the possibility of us sinning by shacking; or both. Despite OUR (he and I) cohabitation plans, I could not have a key to the house and could only come in and out of the house when he was there. That would have been semi *ok*. But then the *monkey wrench* was thrown into the scenario, with one key factor. She wanted me to pay ¼ of the mortgage. *Please note: I didn't expect to stay and not pay for anything.* But the terms were unrealistic and not fair to me at all. So you know this arrangement didn't last long. I was ending up on the short end of the deal. No key, limited entry and I had to pay monetarily, and sexually. Yep time to go. I moved into the first apartment that I could afford and get approved for and he and I eventually broke up. I still kinda believe that he was mad at me for being able to have my independence from his momma. He could have too…if he wanted it. His mother was married and lived with his father in the same house. Years, later when the guy contacted me on Facebook because he was being taken to court for child support and wanted my help in verifying the time frame of our relationship; his mother had passed and although now totally justified in my opinion-he was still living at home with his dad. This means he has officially never lived on his own our outside of his parent's home. Does that mean that he may not be able to function on his own in life outside of his parent's assistance? Again, it is perfectly fine for a man to love and have a relationship with his mother/family. But a man should still be taught how to live a successful life outside of his family's assistance. If he is too dependent on others helping him then he won't understand how to survive. This is similar to when I hear someone say "you can lead a horse to water but you cannot make them drink". Applied here and to me it would mean-*We can only help a man find his purpose-we can't force him to live in it!*

Chapter 7
Pushed Too Far

I have been guilty of *smoochin'* a man multiple times to see how much he would let me *get away* with before he would *snap* and hit me back. Other than my ex *"husband"* there hasn't been a man to hit me back. I've been pushed, had my wrist grabbed, hair pulled; given evil looks; warned about putting my hands on a man and the consequences that could happen afterwards; threatened with the before mentioned as retaliation and all by men…but never hit. I jokingly will say to a man "you don't want any of this" or "don't make me fight you or whip your tail". But I am not dumb enough to actually mean my threats or really act on them. All because I did once and only once other than self-defense from being a victim of domestic violence relationships.

One night I went to a neighbourhood club named Uptown Bar and Grill and while in there I noticed a guy named Donald but I called Franchize whom I had been *seeing*, showing interest in another girl. I was jealous because he and I had the *benefits* of a relationship, just without any titles or commitments. After the club we were both drunk. It happened in the middle of Monroe Street – near the corner intersection of Edmondson Avenue and Monroe Street in Baltimore City – a busy street. Because of the alcohol, I can only vaguely remember what happened. However, I do remember him saying *something* and then I either smooched or slapped him…my immediate reaction was *oh crap (censored) he is going to kill me.* I just knew that his reaction was going to physically beat me up by punching me back out of self-defense, and as a natural reaction. But he exercised self-control and didn't respond. Years later we talked about and laughed about what happened especially once I admitted to him that I *was* really scared. He admitted that he wanted to retaliate but his upbringing would not allow him to do so…thank God! Besides the Bible says in Proverbs 25:28 *A Man without self-control is like a city broken in to and left without walls.* I am glad that even without him knowing about this Bible verse he exercised self-control and restraint.

I wouldn't dare do it again to any man and press my luck and push a man too far from a safe zone because the next time it could end *another* way. Plus now I no longer see the point of being abusive to a man. I just want to love, help and cherish a man and treat him like the king that he is.

There is a reason why we should try not to provoke and push a man too far, and that reason is that he is taught to defend and protect. That includes himself. But if we do decide and challenge a man – why do we get mad when he finally retaliates, and beat our *behinds*? In a way, we asked for it. Now if you know anything about me, then you know that I do not condone domestic violence. However, if you are smacking, smooching, pushing, pinching, poking, kicking, biting, punching or throwing things at a man, because of his natural nature to defend and protect what is his – that includes his personal space, feelings and body, don't be surprised if he defends himself and does it back to you. Don't look shocked or call the police. **YOU MADE HIM DO IT!** If and when the two of you are in the middle of a heated argument, the best thing to do is to let him walk away. When he does walk away, and take a *breather*, he is able to regain self-control of himself and the situation. As he does, he really is still operating in his respective position and **BEING A MAN**, by protecting you from him hurting you. Even the toughest man on the outside is like an Oreo cookie because he still has a heart. Men are tough on the outside like the hard part of the Oreo cookie; but still have feelings and emotions too; similar to the soft creamy inside part of the cookie.

Males were made by God to be stronger creatures physically, emotionally, and I do believe mentally. Women were created to be more emotionally and weaker…not lesser…weaker and submissive. Wait, there is that word that we as women do not like to hear or adhere to-submission. Submission is not a sign of weakness; it's a sign of being in decency and order. There is a lot less confusion in a relationship when a woman can love and honour her man, and he feels important to her. Although many men have adopted the phrase *happy wife- happy life* I do believe that if your man is happy with you, there is nothing and I do mean nothing that he will not do for you. He will be your man, and you his lady. Now I am not saying that everything will be perfect. But a lot of unnecessary arguments and situations may be avoided because you aren't arguing, bickering or even trying to be *the man* (or in a man's role) in the relationship. Encourage him to continue to love you the best way that **HE** can love you which should be the best way that **HE** knows how to love you. Appreciate his efforts and he may be willing to learn additional ways. Allow him to love you with a balance of his best and your needs and make sure that you aren't over needy. In return, you have to allow him to learn and meet your needs and be willing to receive his best. If he feels accepted then he will try hard to love you and make changes in his life for his better which may make your relationship better. Can you love him based on his love alone?

You should have standards and expectations but make sure that your motives are pure and that you are "over expecting his love". *Husbands, love your wives, even as Christ also loved the church, and gave himself for it.* (Ephesians 5:25). Jesus Christ loves us so much that He gave his life and died for us. There should not be anything that your man should not want to do for you, the relationship, and the love that you two share. So your man should love you so much that he is willing to die for you. In other words there is nothing that he should not want to do for you within reason and means. What is it gonna take to make you happy and to be in love with him? While he is discovering that, you should be discovering what makes and keeps him happy and in love with you. Do not allow your past hurts to be blessing blockers to your relationship. Make sure that you do not continuously lash out; curse him out or invoke pain on to him because of your hurt and pains.

Remember hurting people…hurt people.

XII.

Governmental Perfection/Authority:

Stop Flaunting

Chapter 8
Make the Money Don't Flaunt It

The Equal Pay Act of 1963 of the Constitution of the United States of America granted woman fair rights when it comes to employment. Since then, I truly believe that women have worked extremely hard to earn the same or more monetary compensation, for the work that we contribute to a company or business. Historically, males typically hold "harder" jobs, which require more "manual" labour. Isn't it ironic that the label given to jobs which are more physically demanding is called "*man-uall*" labour?

I was listening to Dr. Bill Winston's message on TV one day and he taught that a man's job was to go out and get food because he is physically stronger. While doing so he would risk his life. When he got home his wife would honor him for risking his life to provide food and shelter for his family. I think that that is where the phrase *bring home the bacon* comes from-a man bringing home the pig or whatever other food. In return he honors his wife because she had his children and took care of the household. In today's day and age these roles are no longer separate but the basic instructions still exist in the Bible.

Likewise, ye wives, be in subjection to your own husbands; that, if any obey not the word, they also may without the word be won by the conversation of the wives; While they behold your chaste conversation coupled with fear. Whose adorning let it not be that outward adorning of plaiting the hair, and of wearing of gold, or of putting on of apparel; But let it be the hidden man of the heart, in that which is not corruptible, even the ornament of a meek and quiet spirit, which is in the sight of God of great price. For after this manner in the old time the holy women also, who trusted in

God, adorned themselves, being in subjection unto their own husbands: Even as Sara obeyed Abraham, calling him lord: whose daughters ye are, as long as ye do well, and are not afraid with any amazement. Likewise, ye husbands, dwell with them according to knowledge, giving honour unto the wife, as unto the weaker vessel, and as being heirs together of the grace of life; that your prayers be not hindered (1 Peter 3: 1-7).

Let's face it, men spend more time getting dirty, using physical strength and working harder; and until more recent years - these types of jobs required minimal education and skill. All of this, while women on the other hand do more "pretty jobs" of an administrative nature to include answering phones, typing, filing etc. In the past, women took typing classes and administrative training classes, to increase their knowledge in these fields of employment. I personally believe that men were still protecting us by keeping us clean and safe. Now let me put a stop in this before we go any further, with this side bar. I'm not saying that any job field is greater or lesser than the other or that either gender can't do either type of job. The above situations are simply me speaking from a general stereotypical society standpoint. Anyway, the question to ask your self is-*are my standards realistic expectations and reasons for the choice that I made in my career? Why am I working? What do I hope to accomplish? Am I working for a short term pay check or working towards having a career? Should I learn as much as I can before I start my own business?*

Men get jobs to get money. Women should get jobs to help men provide. I know this statement probably made you just question me and say *what in the world?* But its true once you are married, it's no longer your money for just you but the money you earn is so that you can be a contributor to the household-especially if it needed. Even if your man can afford to take care of the house and he doesn't make you pay any bills, contributing anyway may relived some of his stress and strain. Your check can also go in to a savings account for a rainy day fund; vacations, etc. It's ok to treat yourself but be frugal. Being frugal and versatile is a great and winning combination. One way that I am versatile is in the business world and at home. At home I'm just me and what you see is what you get. But while during business I am *who is required* to get the business done. I am a balance between ghetto and professional and I joke about being able to go from *Becky (professional and proper) to Bonqueesha (hood or everyday as if to my peers)* in zero point two seconds. With that being said, I can relate to many people from many backgrounds in corporate and chill environments. I speak in the voice that is mandated at that time. For example when I am on the phone talking business, depending on who is on the receiving end of my conversation, I speak either proper or urban. Not that I am being racist or anything, I have just learned that people relate better to what is familiar to them. Therefore the *Becky to Bonqueesha* isn't race specific it is message intended specific based on the need. The ability to be versatile shows some level of education and that a woman can be sexy and smart. Some men find a woman who has things going on for her and a good head on her shoulders attractive and sexy. Therefore they prefer a woman to sound educations and professional instead of like an uneducated *hood rat.*

However, men who aren't striving towards accomplishing goals, or making moves to advance themselves, and/or who have become ok with living *day-to-day*, aren't going to understand that you may be trying to better yourself. (On a side note: be weary of a guy who never completes anything to include but not limited to school; has only short term or no employment history, and short relationship spans. He may have a problem with commitments, or he is not going to understand when you are tired or have to go to bed early or just *not in the mood,* or that you can't always hang out late. Because he has idle time to waste, he expects for you to have the same. You have to stay focused and understand that this may not be the man for you. It is one thing for him to be experiencing tuff times but it's another thing for him to be lazy, unmotivated, and unproductive and have no desire to do anything, especially if you two are cohabitating, with his life. If you are the only one working and taking care of the household then it is time for him to go. This type of man is only going to hold you back and/or bring you down if he doesn't display a desire to be in his role as a man. (On a side note: a man who always wants to hang out with his boys and has many excuses as to why he can't go to work has his priorities out of order and obviously too immature for a relationship regardless of his age.

With so many different financial factors, combined with a company's desires of their ideal employee for a position, there has been a shift in economics. Some companies secretly prefer to still hire women for certain administrative roles, and men for labour roles. And with those role preferences, and with the recent turn of the economy, more qualifications are being put on both males and females, regardless of the job industry. Many people in general are willing to take any job that they can get to earn money. This may also lead to a woman getting a job quicker and possibly making more money than her spouse.

You may make more money than your man, but don't flaunt it. Do not allow your financial asset to become a liability in your relationship. Let him still feel like and be the man that you want to love, and respect him to be. It's ok to show him that you have his back and are willing to work with him, but don't continuously slap him over the head with your pay check. Contrary to what some people believe you are not more of a woman (or provider) because you make more money that your mate. There is an old cliché that states that *money can't buy you happiness.* That would explain why so many rich people end up on drugs; as alcoholics; and/or commit suicide. If a couple can work together when the finances are most strained, and finds ways to be happy, I believe that if and when financial blessings do come, that they will not only enhance their relationship but cushion the happiness…much like makeup on most woman's faces. It's supposed to enhance not replace a woman's natural beauty.

It's a wonderful thing to work "x" amount of hours and know that "x" amount of money will be allotted to me on payday. It's a strange thing to tell a man that I have a job and that is all that I am going to have in life. No career in mind or no goals. For me, I have already outline goals as the book of Habakkuk 2:2 says to *write the vision and make it plain.* We can state our dreams but men need proof. Some women say that they are working towards achieving their goals. But they are merely *spitting game* back at the guys or competing to impress the guy. Yep ladies, a bunch of us act as though we have potential to be career and goal oriented aka successful; *and play the role* very well and then *flip the script.* Some of us may try to put on a façade in order to get a man and then reveal our true selves. However, there are many of us who are serious about being successful in life. We (myself included) are determined to achieve or dreams and goals and to fulfil our life's purpose and plan. God predestined us to be successful, have wealth *and the LORD shall make thee the head, and not the tail; and thou shalt be above only, and thou shalt not be beneath; if that thou hearken unto the commandments of the LORD thy God, which I command thee this day, to observe and to do them:* (Deuteronomy 28:13) before we were even formed in our mother's wombs. *"Before I formed you in the womb I knew you, before you were born I set you apart; I appointed you as a prophet to the nations." (Jeremiah 1:5 NIV)*

I've actually had problems with guys not believing that I am working towards my goals and therefore they didn't believe in me or my dreams because of their past experiences with females; combined with the fact that women have tried to *bamboozle* the men. Once some of the males actually *got wind* of me actually achieving some of these goals and being on the right track towards achieving them, they have come back and started declaring their feelings towards me and being *mushy.* But I truly feel some kinda way about this. *If you cannot stick around while I am working towards my goals, why do you*

43

expect that you will be able to reap the benefits of my hard work. I call this the *crab in a barrel* mentality. In other words, when I have seen live crabs in a barrel, there are those crabs which work hard to climb out of it. However, there are those crabs that have made an effort to take the easy route and instead of them making an effort to dig their claws into the barrel sides and work to manoeuvre through the other crabs, the *lazy* crabs simply climb on top of the hard working crabs who are struggling to get out and go over the top and eventually the lazy crabs get to the top of or out of the barrel before the hard working crabs. I prefer not to have a man, who wants to sit around and *walk the red carpet,* or spend the money or eat up my food or live in my house, or drive my car. Instead, help me help myself. If you see that my car needs fixing…offer to help me with the maintenance. If trash needs to be taken out at my house…please feel free to take it to the dumpster. I'm not saying I can't do it on my own…but show me that you at least are willing to meet me half way show me that you are a man whom if need be I can rely on and who has my back…I guarantee that I will do the same with and for you.

I have personally dated men who look at me as being beneath them and they acted as though they had everything going for them. Then misfortune like them losing their job, or going to jail caused them to become humble. All of a sudden they want to become loyal and work together as a team. Some men look down at us until they have to look up to us or to their side and see us there. In other words, I always say that I want a man who is on my level or higher. A man who has (or is trying to) accomplished what I have or more. That way if he has more I am pushed and encouraged to get more and vice versa. However, if he does have more than what I have I don't expect for him to look down at me for not achieving my goals yet. This is especially true if he is older. I mean if he is older that means that he has had more time on earth to do so and make accomplishments-*right*?

Anyway, a man may treat you like garbage until he sees that the grass is not greener on the other side but fake and artificial turf. At that point if you have been a good girl all along, he should realize just that. But be aware he may not be your *good* guy. He may not realize how good of a woman that you are until he has been humbled and lost everything. Don't gloat. You have to remain humble. Humility is the key to getting more in life. Arrogance can be a quick and devastating down fall like when the bible says *thine heart was lifted up because of thy beauty, thou hast corrupted thy wisdom by reason of thy brightness: I will cast thee to the ground; I will lay thee before kings, that they may behold thee.* (Ezekiel 28:17). I once heard someone say that "the grass only looks greener on the other side because they are watering and taking care of it". A man should be willing to appreciate your financial status and be motivated to make progressions in his own life.

Now another side to you flaunting your pay status is that with the wrong guy he may try to keep his money for what he wants to use it for, and drain your finances. With these types of men once he feels that he has gotten everything that he can from you, he will leave you alone. So now you are risking being alone, and broke, and left thinking *if I had only kept my financial status to myself.* I used to say *what's mine is mine and what's his is mine* which was a play on the phrase *what is yours is mine and what's mine is yours.* But I stopped using it as often to avoid appearing greedy. I also learned from one of Dr. Bill Winston's messages that what Jesus being the Son of God gets, we as humans because we are joint heirs to the kingdom of God also get based on Romans 8:17 *And if children, then heirs; heirs of God, and joint-heirs with Christ; if so be that we suffer with him, that we may be also glorified together.* Additionally what a man in a relationship gets a woman gets.

If you are dealing with and/or involved with someone who has the mentality that they will always take from you and are not willing to give back to you or as I like to say *pour back into you* – when you tried to have his back – then it's time to move on. You can't help everyone. (Oh, on a side note, please do not let a man who has less than you validate what you have and/or have accomplished. He may try to transfer his low self-esteem and/or feelings of being inadequate to you but that does not mean that you have to accept the transfer).

I had a guy who did not have a car, tell me that my car wasn't the best looking car or in his words *looks like something a foreigner would drive*. Again, he did not have a car or even a driver's license. There were guys who put down my home because it wasn't fully furnished. Sometimes some of the things that guys were saying in judging my possessions were hurtful and made me consider trying to get things which were pleasing to them instead of taking my time and securing things in my time and when I could afford them.

Today, I have learned to live a life of wisdom. If I can't afford it, I don't act like I can. If I have to take my time and save up money to make a purchase –I do. No more pretending that *I have it like that* especially when there are times that I don't. Why? Because I have seen some people who are considered *upper class* walk around with holes in their clothes; shop at the thrift store, and ride the bus. They were confidant in who they were and were outside of *people bondage*. Who cares about what someone else thinks about or portrays? I continue to do the best that I can, and strive for what I dream and desire to have.

Ok so we have discussed the fact that you may make more money than your man. And we discussed not flaunting it. But now let's talk about the woman who needs to be introduced to her worth because she tends to spend money *buying* her man. Please, please, please get reintroduced to your value and worth. You cannot buy a man with your money – or your *coochie credit card* aka your vagina! Yep I said it and the way it needed to be said. Engage his mind and your conversations may attract his interest. When you go out – especially in the beginning stages he is supposed to pay to court you. Let him be the man. Now I'm not saying that over some time, and from time to time that you can't offer to *treat* him, but balance between being a *gold digger* and a *doormat*. It is one thing to work with him in a collective effort but it's another thing for him to *bank on* your money. Before I go on maybe I should define what *courting is…* to me courting means that a man is trying to pursue the opportunity of exploring his possibility and to do whatever he can to establish a relationship and win your heart. Now there is a genuine courting and lustful courting although one can become the other. You may have a nice figure and then he becomes more intrigued with your mind more or vice versa. Allow yourself to be courted. Once you trust him AFTER you have been courted initially then it's ok to at least offer to pay. But there are rules.

Now when it comes to a woman offering to treat please know that genuine *MAN LAW* has a 3-to-4 rule when dealing with us.

For every offer:

Part I: It *is* ok for a woman to offer.

Part II. In a man's mind an offer goes a long way and could cause him to appreciate you more in the long run. And because he appreciates the fact that the relationship is not one sided and of no benefit to him, he may show more frequent signs of his appreciation.

Part III. If and when you do offer and if and when he does accept your offer, he has to figure out if he has to be mindful of the amount of money that he spends; or is he going to be reprimanded for spending too much or not paying back the full amount? *Did she really mean her offer? Was it sincere or was it a means of her trying to control me and the relationship?* These are some of the thoughts, which may cross his mind.

I've been guilty of trying to *help out* a guy when I was involved with him, by putting *MY* money from *MY* purse in his pocket or wallet when we went out, as if he was *footing* the bill. This to give the illusion and perception to others that *MY* man is paying, and has money *like that*. Honestly, in the back of my mind, I was keeping a calculation of monies spent and hoping that he'd return my change. Sometimes the guys did sometimes they didn't. I'm just being real. Then on another instance, I had a *boyfriend* who needed $40.00 until his payday. I went to the ATM machine and gave it to him. On his payday he gave me $50.00 back. He said that the extra $10.00 was because he never had anyone give him money before. I honestly pray that the next guy who am I involved in a serious relationship with is financially stable so that he and I can participate in a combined financial effort and not have to stress over our finances. In fact, one of my long term goals after marriage is that I want us to be able to pay someone to pay our bills so that we will not have to be bothered with having to see the bills themselves. For real, can you imagine life without having to look at a bill or debt collection notice?

Part IV: Also according to *MAN LAW* men want to ask you when they need help, but it's against their rules. Just like with other laws of the land that we live in, laws tend to get broken and there are exceptions to a man asking us for help. Men who are trying to be *real men* or in their place as a man will do everything that they can to NOT ask a woman for help. He may do whatever he can to get money before he asks us. Although I don't condone selling drugs aka *hustlin'*, after observing the reason behind the concept-I now have a better understanding from men about why they had to consider this an option. For some men they hustle out of the love and greed for money. (I'm not talking about you in this section of this book). I'm talking about the man who has such a strong desire to provide for his family and himself, and either he doesn't have a job or his job is not sufficient enough that he will *hug the block* (stay outside all night selling drugs) from sun down to sun up to make sure that his babies have food, clothes, pampers and all of their needs are met. Honestly at first I didn't understand and I judged. Then I became educated. Their fathers and role models taught some of these men *"the game of survival"*. Some may have begun as *hustlers* to provide. Then the money started coming more frequently and with or without a jail visit. Some men became addicted to the *drug of selling drugs*; the money and got greedy. Others were able to walk away from the drug selling game. After speaking with some of these guys, (on both sides of the greed issue) I do believe that if they could have gotten legitimate jobs they would have chosen not to sell drugs. Again I'm not talking about men who are greedy or lazy! They just liked the excitement and validation of the identity that they wanted to be perceived as by selling drugs, like a thug, hoodlum or unafraid individual and not a punk. But I am talking about those who found their *"back up against the wall"* with little-to no options or help for their situations like Darnell. Let's get back to the point of this section in this chapter.

Here's an idea-if you see that your man is in need and you know that he will not directly accept money from you – be creative. Try leaving a card where he would least expect it with the money in it; drive his car and fill up his gas tank; or let our husband be your *private dancer* and *tip him.* Again be creative! He will reward you for it.

However, be weary of a man who always has his *hand out*, in your pocketbook (or your refrigerator). If there is no return on your investment it is time to change your *investment options.*

Are we too much woman for him…

weight or attitude wise?

The bottom line is that no matter what, you have to *fall back* and stay in your position. A man has to be allowed to *be the man*. Let him make an attempt to figure out a situation before you try to send him a life line. I like to use this example: sit on the beach's shore as he goes out into the depth of the ocean. If he feels that he is beginning to drown him will swim back to shore and ask for a life jacket before returning to the ocean again. Again, stay on the shore and wait for him to ask for the life jacket. Be his partner and ready, rested and available for him to come to as a resource. If he *tags you in handle your business.* He will appreciate the fact that he knows that if HE NEEDS TO he can count on you.

He wants you in his life not needs you!

Lastly and as a general rule of thumb-if he can't afford to date you-he may not be able to afford to marry you.

Chapter 9
I Don't Need A Man

Why do I need a man? I have my own job; car, business, a network of contacts; no children and I have my own place. Who pays my bills? Me! If I am handling my business on my own (for the most part), what could a man really do for or offer me? Companionship? I have a cat name Gabby who shows me normal human-animal affection. I am INDEPENDENT and cannot see myself as labelled I-Am-Dependent on a man!

Nice try; however I read somewhere that there is a MALE inside of every FEMALE. (Oh stop it and bring your mind back this way). There is the word FEMALE which contains the word MALE; MRS. contains the word MR. and SHE contains HE.

The words most men don't want to hear a woman say and no matter how much they may deny it are *I don't need a man!* It is a very rare case to hear a hetero sexual man say that he does not need or want a woman, because every man ultimately wants one woman to settle down with and marry. If he does it could be that he is guarding his heart while blocking the possibilities of his feelings being hurt and his heart from being broken. Once again, he is being a protector-this time to and of himself. He also wants to protect you and his family.

The way that I see it is that we as women may have accomplished some things in life and have finally achieved some of our goals, but we don't want a man to come along and distract us from being focused on our careers, bills, children etc. and risk losing everything that we have worked so hard to accomplish and obtain. Men, we don't want a man who is going to come along and take away from and/or destroy what we have worked diligently to build and establish on our own, especially if we have had to start over multiple times. I'm not saying that we don't want to establish and build these things *with* you. However, if you are not around, please don't expect our goals, destiny and success to wait on your arrival. You should want a woman who is at least trying to have something to offer rather than just sex? She may have the missing elements and materialistic things that you are missing and/or needing-especially if she has her own place and you still live at home with your family or roommates. Wouldn't it be good to have option?   One thing for sure - two things for certain; God created everything in the world to have some type of mate. Why else would God take the time to create the Earth's CREATURES and their mates and make sure that they are compatible? As I mentioned in Chapter I, he even took the time to make a special compatible mate for His human creation-Adam.

So many times, we tell God that we want in a man, but we don't ask God for any type of special request. Here's what I mean: when I go and patron a restaurant, I may inquire as to the possibility of and then either request something that is not the menu or that something on the menu be customized, so that it accommodates my preference. For example, my steak has to be cooked *very* well done, so that there is no sign that that animal ever lived or had a heartbeat. This means that it has to stay in the oven (or be processed) longer than some else's steak who desires to have their steak cooked medium rare or rare. But my steak is not kept in the oven so long, that it is over cooked and ruined. It is kept in the cooking process long enough to be exactly what I want and desire.

What's wrong with going to God and placing a specific order for our mate? Customized and just how we would like for him to be well done and ready?

A man may or may not be attracted to an independent type of woman. But we have to be careful not to let our independence over power our desire, to be in a successful relationship. To take it one step further, it shouldn't replace our placement as the woman in the relationship. If you chose, be a woman who is independent. However, be flexible and open to a man's contributions to you and your life; Men, remember that we want a compatible companion, who is going to be *the man*, and the one who God kept for us until it was time for us to meet and enter into a relationship with the hopes of it leading to marriage. Not someone who wants us to erase our identity, which then allows them to mold us like a ball of clay into only what and who they want us to become. Clay-if not properly taken care of-eventually dries out and becomes hard. Once clay is dry and gets hard, it no longer has a use, and therefore gets thrown away, if the soft and flexible clay wasn't made first into something beautiful. That is how a man should want his woman: flexible, useful, and what he considers beautiful. Not hard hearted, dry, useless, inflexible, overly independent and being of no use to he or any other man-so then they will have the option of throwing us away.

We don't truly want to be with a man with whom there is a chance that we may lose our own identity entirely. Men, encourage us to be your *helpmate* and the woman who is confident enough to go out work, and contribute to the household. And then when it is time for us to spend some *me money* there should not be a problem. *Me Money* could mean money used to get our hair and/or nails done; a new outfit, perfume etc. or something else that we desire…you know the things that we do to make and keep ourselves attractive to and for you or something that we desire. If you are blessed it may even be used to buy something for you without using the household money.

We need you to love, protect pray for and motivate us. Please *push* us to be the best women that we can be. This in turn will benefit you as we are successfully in our lane as your woman. Nurture us as you would a flower and allow us to grow and become all that we can be. In other words no matter how much we try and deny it-we need a man in our life; otherwise God would not have created men.

I want to close this chapter with one of my favourite stories of the bible which is about Ruth. Ruth was a widower who decided to dedicate her life to her late husband's mother. She even moved back to her mother-in- law's home land and was taking care of her mother-in-law. While gathering food she was discovered by Boaz the owner of the land in which she was gathering the left overs of his servants. To sum it all up- Boaz redeemed Ruth. Ruth no longer had to eat scraps but could eat plenty. Boaz eventually married her. Ruth could have been like some of us and been content with settling for the lack but instead she opened up her heart and life to Boaz, who did I mention was rich! So how many of you are now waiting on your Boaz type of man in the sense of him being a redeemer and being rich is a bonus? Have you opened up your heart and life after being hurt to be loved properly or are you content with being in lack of love and finances?

XIII.

Rebellion, Depravity:
Nice Guys Finish Last

Chapter 10
Nice Guys Do Have to Finish Last –
They Really Do

In August 1996, I began my freshman year of college. I decided to enjoy my new found freedom of pre-adulthood. Although I did eventually earn a degree, which took me five years instead two point five because I skipped classes, under aged drank and more. I still graduated from Prince George's Community College in Largo, MD.

When I should have been in class, I hung out with the *cool* kids like Churchill (whose nickname is Church), Rob, Jovan, Warren, Brandon, Steve, Duck and others; and we played Spades majority of the day in the game room. On some days we attended class during the day, but later we went "clubbing" at night. That year I met quit a few guys who were really *mature* for me and some who I turned my nose up to because they weren't as attractive or what I considered (at that time) my type. However, it wouldn't be until years later after I graduated college that I would fully learn, and understand my desired attributes of a mate, suitable for me or my type.

The first of the two nice guys, who I wish I had the opportunity to meet now to apologize, was a guy whose name was Howard but we called by his nickname of *Duck. Duck* hung out in the rec area on campus in between the bookstore and Jerry's in a room with an old piano I think it was called The Den and it was similar to *The Pit* on the popular TV show *A Different World*, whereas college students and high school students from the neighbouring school ate, hung out, chilled and created. He wore his hair in orange twist, which looked like he was beginning to grow dreds. His body build was thinner than I liked, and his wardrobe primarily consisted of a blazer and whatever he wanted to wear under it which mostly was a t-shirt. It was not necessarily the latest fashion style; but it was a style of his own. We connected primarily because like me he also played the piano, keyboard and sang.

Although I was naive about *Duck's* intentions towards me, he made it perfectly clear. For one of my birthdays, he coordinated with one of my favourite professors (Professor Frederick Fair), my fellow classmate and friend Brandon, and a couple of students to get me to come to one of the activities rooms. When I opened the door to the room, he had rose pedals leading from the door's entrance, to a chair and on the areas surrounding the chair. There were flowers and a cake. He had planned and thrown me a surprise birthday party. After the festivities were over, I thanked him and got a ride home from school with Brandon. Wait my defense, Duck did not drive and I didn't feel like the long two bus ride to get home. Plus Brandon and I were secretly dating, even though no one on campus knew or could confirm it.

Years later we ran into each other, and Duck had gotten very sexy. *Where did all of his confidence and swag come from all of a sudden?* Duck and I hung out together a couple of times but not for long because I had begun dating and eventually married my *ex-husband* and soon after we lost contact. One day Duck called me just before he was about to move to Atlanta and he begged me to meet him. I declined him once again trying to love me and I truly believe that he wanted me to finally let him into my heart. But because I was married, I said *No!* But I have to be honest and say that me saying no was not just because I was married but because I didn't realize our potential to have a future. Due to all that was going on including domestic violence and abuse I should have ended my *marriage* and allowed my *ram in the bush* similar to in Genesis 22:9-13 when God allowed a ram to be sacrificed instead of Abraham's son, to save me. Duck could have been the man to save me and my heart from the hurt and pain of being in a crazy and abusive marriage. Since I became single/unmarried, I have looked for him but as of the time of this book's original manuscript being completed still no avail. However, making additional edits on later drafts, I met Duck again and this time he was married. He looked tired, worn down and unhappy. Oh this time he tried again to sway me to be with him but as a *side chick*. Duck shared with me the fact that he thought that his wife had committed adultery and is pregnant with twins that are possibly not his. Anyway, thinking back if my choices were different, our lives and decisions may have been different, like him changing his mind about moving to Atlanta or maybe asking me to move with him and I would have gone. If I had only listened to his heart...

Now the other guy named Rick, I met was in my English 101 class and he wore glasses, and drove a Nissan Pulsar which he says was burgundy. I swear that it was orange and we used to laugh and go back and forth with the discussion of it occasionally, after we were adults, and many years later. He gave me a ride home a lot of days because at that time I was a faithful bus rider. In the beginning of the semester, he let me borrow an ink pen which I never according to him returned (see I acknowledged it lol). It was not until I got older that I realized that at the age of 18 when I met him, I was still on road to discovering my ideal mate. I was immature, naïve, and really had no clue. So when he called me on the phone I would place him on three-way calls with another female. He still was trying to be my boyfriend when he did call me on the phone, but I ignored his interest and eventually he and the other female later developed a relationship, and had a daughter together. Once I saw how well he treated her and acted in their relationship, I became extremely jealous because the guy whom I had become pregnant didn't believe that I was pregnant until after I had the abortion. I was mad that I had gotten pregnant by the other guy and not Rick. Anyway even after his daughter's mother and I were no longer friends, he and I still remained friends –even until today. He would share with me the good and the *bads* about their relationship, as well as relationships he had with other women. I shared with him my *ups and downs* of dating, and I would even tell the guys

I've dated about my *best male friend Rick.* I told him not too long ago that he was the reason that I'm still single. He said "Why"? I said, "I don't know". But in all actually the truth is that guys whom I have dated say that they have seen the depth of feelings that I had towards Rick and Rick towards me. Years later we met in person again after talking on the phone for some time, and he had on some nice jeans, a black skirt, and some nice non-nerdy glasses. We always had the type of relationship whereas we would talk about everything and I tease him and say that I tell him WAYYYY tooo much. Throughout the years he proved not only to be a good friend, but one of my best friends and I found myself attracted to him. The funny thing is that I do care about Rick and always will but since we have not been together in a committed relationship after almost twenty years of knowing each other, I have come to the conclusion that it will probably never happen. We discussed being in a relationship with one another, but can't ever seem to be on the *same page at the same time,* or be ready at the same time to be committed to one another. It's best he and I remain nothing more than friends. Especially since he says repeatedly (until recently) that he will never get married to anyone. At first I thought that he was just joking around, but after him saying it on a consistent basis, I believe him. I believe that he is either never going to get married or just has no intentions of marrying me. I am perfectly ok with him and me not getting married and if he does finally get married to the lady whom he recently told me that he was thinking about marrying, I honestly and wholeheartedly wish them the best.

Nice guys sometimes blow their opportunity to finish first or last. This is why the Bible says *not to be unequally yoked (*2 Corinthians 6:14*).* A guy may have a heart of gold and treat us nice. But we as women tend to walk over those men with a good heart for the mean thug type of guys, or the ones who don't treat us well. We ignore the guys who truly care about us and tend to be attracted to the guys who are cheap, selfish and who obviously care more out themselves than they do about us. Is that because we like the challenge of trying to convert the thug with our vivid imagery concept that our *stuff (*vagina) is *that good*...so good that we can change his ways? Or is it that we don't feel as though we deserve a guy with a golden heart?

Ladies, the ideal man for me is a combo of treating me well with respect, honour and love, and being able to protect our family and home, all while loving and respecting God first. He has to be able to have a relationship with God (not just a knowledge of him) and then with me. Also he will be willing and able to understand and love me unconditionally. This doesn't have to be done just materialistically but from his heart. My ideal mate will be willing to give and reciprocate my love or more than my love back to me genuinely.

Men, I can't say it enough. Women have been through a lot. Not saying that you haven't but I've only been and will only be a woman all my life. Some of these situations have caused us to be tougher and stronger than many of us have expected or truthfully wanted to have to be in life. Many of us have had to be the provider, protector, and more; the roles men typically hold. We still want to be treated *nicely* and as women, and we like when we can play our position and stay in our lanes/roles as women.

There was a time once when I had a man tell me that I was too strong. With all that I've been through – is that possible? How am I supposed to be? I refuse to go back to being timid, frail, and gullible or naïve. Yet, I still have my heart open to be receptive to the love of a man and to eventually acquire and maintain a successful relationship.

Chapter 11
It's Just the Way It Is

No matter how much we try to fight it – the man is still in charge! I'm sorry ladies…*that's just the way it is*. And if we are honest with ourselves, for a lot of things they need to be that way because women tend to handle things wayyyyyy too emotionally.

If the foundations be destroyed, what can the righteous do? (Psalm 11:3). *The quality of the foundation determines the degree of stability of the relationship.* (Dr. Bill Winston). God's biblical order for family is that a man is the head of the family. No he is not the only one with a voice in a relationship or family, but that final decisions (once discussed with his spouse) are to be made by him. Especially, if a decision is complicated and the spouses are having difficulties coming to a conclusion or agreement. It is best for a man to hear from God so that he can make the best and correct choice. Not only is a man the decision maker of the family, he is the provider, and protector of the family. A wife is his backbone, and shoulders. She is to be the one who manages the house, and the children. The children and grandchildren are the toes and the fingers. We have to remember that although the head is connected to the backbone/spine the backbone/spine is not always visible, but it still supports the head which houses the brain. The brain is the control of the body. It serves a vital organ in the body's functions, mobility and stability. A body can function with a dysfunctional or semi functional or damaged brain but I have never seen someone (other than on movies) with their head on backwards. If there is damage to a person's brain then something else in a person's body is not going to function properly. Everything in life has a purpose and systematic way of functioning. Think about how you brush your teeth; wash your car; brush your hair; put on your socks and shoes; prepare meals; eat meals and the list goes on.

As I mentioned earlier in Chapter 1, this again goes back to the very beginning of the word, according to the Bible. In the book of Genesis, God had made everything, the first human being-Adam. However, everything in creation had a suitable mate except Adam. By the second chapter of Genesis around the 18th verse, God made someone *special* for Adam whom Adam named Eve, by putting Adam to sleep. God opened Adam's chest cavity and took out one of his ribs, in which Eve was formed from. Eve was to be Adam's helper and wife. God did not create Adam from Eve and again Eve was created from Adam-for Adam. When Adam saw her, he was pleased, and said she is the *bone of my bones, and flesh of my flesh (*Genesis 2:23*)* and we must recognize the fact that God created Adam first and then Eve, which created the concept of family, and that order is how it's order was established.

As I stated earlier, a man's role in family is to be a provider and to be the leader. The female's role is to be a helper to her husband, which includes nurturing his children. When a man and a woman get married NETIHER one is to deny the other ANYTHING including sex. (*Do not deprive each other except perhaps by mutual consent and for a time, so that you may devote yourselves to prayer. Then come together again so that Satan will not tempt you because of your lack of self-control.* 1 Corinthians 7:5) There is not supposed to be any separation including bank accounts. *How am I supposed to do that?* First-I need it for my business and second-I am really praying about it but I hope my future mate agrees to us having one joint bank account for the needs of the household and then we can each have our own personal individual account which can be used to cushion the household account. And you belong to one another totally including your bodies. In God's eyes you become one being. However, your soul should belong to God! The answer is that by having all of your bank accounts separate that is not total submission to one another or oneness. You are operating under a "what if _________ happens back up plan" without a cause. Somehow you being the women is still exercising control. When Eve disobeyed God and ate the forbidden fruit of the Garden of Eden in which she and Adam lived in – it caused Adam and Eve to be evicted from the garden. God had gave them specific instruction of NOT TO EAT IT (Genesis 2:17)! If Adam had fulfilled his role, and not allowed Eve to over throw his authority, the family union would not have been distorted because of Eve eating the forbidden fruit and persuading Adam to do the same. Just like with Adam allowing Eve to be in his role as a man many of today's men, have allowed *today's women* to be in theirs. How so? To best explain let's start with this:

We as woman need to really study every book of the Bible. If you are not sure where to start I would recommend the entire book of Genesis; Ephesians 5:22-33; and every book of Proverbs, especially Proverbs 18:22, so that we can clearly have our roles and responsibilities defined, with our mates, and in our lives in general.

Next, do you know that, some men actually feel lost, and out of place when they can't be *in* their place as a provider, and take care of their families? The more that they can't provide for us and their family, the more they feel inadequate, low and as a failure. The worst thing that we as women can do is to *kick our man* while he is down, especially to point that he is almost destroyed. The *best* thing that we can do is encourage him, and show him that you still love, care about, and respect him as man. Reassure him that you are with him for the long haul, and that you aren't disappointed in him and/or going to abandon him and/or label him as a failure.

This maybe one of the few times that it is ok to *fake it until he makes it*, despite what things look like, have and exercise faith. Now this part is extremely important, so please read this carefully!

Part I. if your man is lazy, sits and drinks and/or smokes all day instead of working or looking for work; sleeps most of the day; plays video games; and not giving his best or any effort to make any type of life accomplishments then STOP reading here, and go to the next section of the book. But if he is seriously trying to do something with his life by going to school and or working in a job or in his own company please continue reading here.

This next part may be very difficult for some of you because for a long time it was very hard for me. I couldn't understand the concept of and why this was important. Again, I stress and emphasize-if your man is trying… get in to the practice until it's habitual for you to say something FREQUENTLY to encourage him.

Divert his attention from whatever negative circumstances that he is faced with and help him redirect his focus on the positive things surrounding him. I like to call this *ego stroking*. Things like *baby, it's going to be ok; you are still my baby* and *I know you are trying to handle your business;* can go a long way with, to and for him. And if you really want to make him blush lol the next time he is discussing a decision with you (major or minor), you can quickly lighten the conversation by using these simple nine words: *you are the man and whatever you say goes*. Ladies try to keep a *straight face* and not smile or use too sarcastic of a tone (*wink*). But it will help you to keep the peace and keep your man happy.

Chapter 12
No House Husband

I was once in a relationship with a guy named Thomas once who lived in Ohio. Even though I had already decided that I didn't want to be in a long distance relationship, I still gave him a try. We talked on the phone daily for about four months even though I had met him about four years prior to our constant phone calls, and he had recently become separated from his wife, and my marriage was recently annulled. Eventually during the fourth month he came and visited me, during the weekend that I had an important milestone in my life – my first book signing for my first book *I Married Satan.*

Because, I was so blinded by being love with him, I missed so many important warning signs, to not enter into a relationship with this man. Things like he wasn't financially stable; his *so-called* business wasn't doing as well as he made it seem; and most of all his divorce wasn't final. He also shared with me reasons why he and his wife had separated and made things appear as if *she* just *wild out* and treated him *like a dog.* Conveniently, he forgot to admit to all of the things that he had done to contribute to her *justifications*, for her words and actions. Yes, I do feel now that based on his relationship with me, that he may have pushed her to some of her actions and decisions.

Anyway, when he came and visited, even though I couldn't afford it financially I purchased his bus ticket, and he stayed at my house. He left but three weeks to a month after he came and visited for the first time, he came back and visited again. This time he managed to purchase his *own* ticket to Maryland, and I picked him up once again from the Greyhound bus station in Downtown Baltimore. Because I try to be a responsible adult –I couldn't change my daily routine of working two jobs - Monday-Friday, and then *pushing* my book business during any other time I could. This meant that while he was here visiting, I still had to go to work.

Just before he arrived this time, we discussed transitioning the status of our relationship from boyfriend and girlfriend to husband and wife now that we were both single. Oh, also added to the topic of discussion was the possibility of him one day moving to Maryland to live. But I stressed and over emphasized to him that he would HAVE to HAVE a job, before we could entertain and/or further discuss the idea of him moving here. He then explained that he and his mother had discussed the possibility of him relocating to Maryland to make a *fresh start* in life. Since he was very convincing to me that he was in fact actively searching for a job here, and despite so many gut feelings telling me *no* – I agreed to let him stay at my house to attend multiple job interviews and possible training. This instead of him traveling back and forth to Maryland, and spending more money in commuting. It just seemed to make sense.

Well at first, it was fun and comforting to have him here. Not to mention the fact that it was awesome to come home to a clean house, and a *home cooked meal*- that I didn't have to rush home and cook. And not having to spend money of fast food was awesome and healthier. Too bad it was all temporary.

My-oh my how things began to change for the worse after a few weeks. For example, he claimed to be staying up late and getting up early to persistently apply for jobs by filling out job applications online. He even went as far as to go on a second interview for a *prospective* job. Again, he was very convincing and this lasted for about two more weeks. But just like I always say *the truth will always come to light.* Soon, he began sleeping in late and staying up all night, claiming to be *semi working* a home based business, but abruptly stopped working his planned scheduled hours for his company. Quickly and soon after he began working and searching less for a job and I would come home to find an unmade bed. Then the meals were either thrown together at the last minute or non-existent and not to mention the $80 worth of groceries, which normally lasted me about a month –became obsolete in a matter of days. *If you are home all day chilling then at least why isn't dinner made? I'm bringing home the bacon the least you can do is cook it.* We began to argue constantly and daily, because I had expressed my concern about his excessive use of my house's gas and electricity by keeping the computer on most of the day and night. But he did not care…why should he? Honestly, it probably wouldn't have been as much of a problem if was working and/or making sure that money was coming in to the house-somehow; you know-him giving me a reason to *get off of his back?!* Justifiably, since I had to be the responsible adult in the household, all of the fun times that we were having quickly changed to non-fun and stressful times.

Eventually, what started out as a potentially beautiful and life long relationship, ended in me getting *fed up*. This male is obviously not ready for a relationship and I now see some of the reasons why his marriage didn't work, to include him being lazy. He had mentioned to me that she was tired of being the one who paid all of the bills, and now I totally could relate to her point. The main one being that he is lazy. She and I both were the main and only ones taking care of our respective households. When did it become ok for a man to be taken care of by a woman-other than his mama lol?

After a few weeks of arguing (something that I really don't like to do, because of the joyous state which I am in my life right now), I told him to pack his bags and call his momma. She was going to have to be the one to purchase his transportation to get back home because I wasn't doing it. I had already given and done enough for him. Wait! You may be thinking *you brought him there but you are not going to help him get back?* Nope he paid for that ticket. ABSOLUTELY NOT! You see, I failed to mention that I had also began to feel that he was cheating on me – and guess what? He was! His so called ex-girlfriend and he were still emailing, calling each other with intimate correspondence on SKYPE and Facebook; and he started leaving his phone turned off or downstairs; so they were probably texting each other too. Ok so you are probably thinking that those are all circumstantial and that I had no solid proofs. Well, I am glad and hope that you are thinking that. I found out the facts and I had solid proof, when I sat down at his computer one day and he had his Facebook page open to his messages. The way that Facebook was set up at that time – not only were old messages on his screen between them, but right while I was sitting there, she sent him a message in *real time*! Caught…red handed…in black and white. Also, someone would call the house phone and hang up and/or if answered it, he would claim that it was a telemarketer calling. There were all of a sudden a lot of telemarketers calling on my home phone which was something that almost never happened. So…since I am not someone who "hates" or "blocks" or stands in the way of someone wanting to be with someone else, I released him to go and be with her.

He called and tried to come back and reconcile with me months later, but I had already compromised myself and heart once with him –he didn't deserve another chance. (P.S. I'm not mad at you I wish you and her the best).He didn't want to believe or accept that I was serious at first. However, he eventually deleted me as a friend on Facebook after his ex-wife had befriended me on there was *blowing my Facebook inbox up!* She would send me these ridiculously long, annoying messages. Anyway, he deleting me (and then me deleting and blocking her as well) was cool and perfectly ok since she was getting as my friend Angie says "extra" with it. He and I have since forgiven each other; become and remain friends on Facebook and in person. Ironically now he has a vehicle and was working a job and even blessed me with $50 when I really needed it while I was passing through Ohio.

There have been other guys like Darnell who saw me having my own place as being convenient for them, and the perfect opportunity to move in and take up residence with me.

But they don't want to be in the full position of the *Man of the House*. They want to have all of the benefits of a relationship like the security of having shelter and a place to live; meals etc. without the full responsibility of helping to establish and maintain the household. I definitely have proven that I can maintain my own household without having a "man of the house". Therefore, I do not want or need neither house husband nor do I desire to be a *housewife*. If a man wants to move in with me and cohabitate, first I would like to have a chocolate diamond wedding ring set, marriage license, ceremony and name change (an official one, and you can't be married to anyone else or have a gazillion kids). Our cohabitation will have to be mutually beneficial and we would both have to share responsibilities. We will sit down and discuss our roles, expectations and goals and collectively work towards a successful and meaningful long term relationship.

You game? Are there any takers?

XIV.

Deliverance, Release:

Women's Introspection

Chapter 13
Size Matters

I have a habit of adapting and practicing in my life the saying *if a man can accept me at my worse-then he will appreciate me at my best*. So the first couple of times that I hang out with a new prospective guy, I make sure that my hair is decent, my outfits are cute, and that I am wearing nice performed body spay, lotion or oil; and that I smell good. After we went out a couple of times and he saw me at my "best" it was time to see if he could handle the *everyday me*. So I would pull my hair in a ponytail instead of flat ironing or styling it, and just throw on something like comfortable sweat pants, jeans or leggings/tights, in an effort to create a less dressy outfit. Then, I try no makeup and/or may not put on body fragrance via lotion or spay (and no I still didn't stink lol). I believe that even on rainy days I can shine and look good, and I dress to make sure that I modify my wardrobe to accommodate the weather. But something as small as to whether or not I look or smell good hasn't been enough to secure and maintain a successful relationship.

Despite me doing my part, within the general dating arena, there seems to be a shift in men's mindset. *What happened to the men who didn't have to be asked to open doors? Who brought flowers, and courted us? When did they get replaced? How did men who no longer see the necessity in doing these things replace them?* Maybe we as women have allowed our values to be reduced to *quickies,* so men no longer see the need to do all of those *old school* things. Have we really let the men we encounter get from *first* to *third* base quickly and without any type of investment except verbal ones? And the sad part is that the lack of courting isn't even based on the ignorance of any age group.

Once upon a time I thought that the older in age that a man got the more mature he got. So that meant that he would have learned how to treat a lady by the time he reached a certain age. Then I started seeing that age really is just a number. Regardless of how old or young a man is his chivalry can be alive if he chooses to practice and perform it no matter how small or extravagant it may be. But we have to do our part as well.

Small things do count. We can't start a relationship cooking, cleaning and keeping ourselves desirable (when possible), and then change; especially abruptly. However, men please read this next part closely DO NOT START OUT SPOILING A WOMAN AND THEN EXPECT TO STOP! Also, men be yourself. If you begin an interaction with a female by putting your best foot forward, she is going to expect better efforts to manifest as the times of your interactions and eventual relationship matriculates. We may have become accustomed to you doing things a certain way and if you change up…well let me explain through this example. If in the beginning of a relationship you allow us to sit home and not work, and then when things get hard and not work as you plan, or if we don't volunteer to *jump in* and start contributing, you get upset because some of us have become lazy and unwilling to help. We get confused when you brag about the fact that you pay all the bills and *take care of your* woman and then make a demand for us to get a job. (Side note: a woman should already be somewhat independent when she meets a man to include a minimum of having a job). So why are you trying to get us up and get a job all of a sudden now? Make up your mind…you say that we aren't being consistent – but we are-based on what we have become used to and based on what you have allowed us to do. We are merely continuing what you started us out doing. (Side note: I make a man feel lucky and blessed to find me, much like finding a hundred dollar bill in a Laundromat or casino. But not all women are good women like me and I would never sit home all day while my man works nor would I allow us to struggle financially because of me not pitching in. I have a habit of offering to help a guy or at least contributing. Then I find out that all men don't keep it honest with me and try and take advantage of my kindness and try to look at me as *a dummy*.) This is why it is important to have conversations about expectations early on in a relationship. Be sure to discuss grooming habits, appearance and the possibility of your or him changing.

Here is a *nugget*/note just for us women: If you have gained weight because of child birth, stress or merely over eating – work on losing it. You will feel better and look better and possibly re-attract your man to you. At least get your feet done. A lot of men love pretty feet. Even if you can't afford to go to the nail shop make an attempt at keeping your feet looking good by giving yourself a pedicure at home. Some men were also taught to look at our hands to see if we take care of ourselves. They figure if we spend time getting our nails done then we spend time caring for our appearance. For some of us, we use our hands pretty frequently so it's hard to keep our nails done. For me, I play the piano and do a lot of writing and work with my hands, so although my nails may not be painted I still spend time trying to keep myself well groomed. But I do love to show off my feet especially since they are *pretty* and I have no corns or bunions...lol. It's more to being a well groomed individual than just being well groomed on the outside of our bodies.

Men want and need the same things that we emotionally and physically need like massages, love notes, tokens of appreciation, a thank you; companionship, honesty, respect, motivation, and someone who listens. Not to mention the opportunity for him to open up to feel wanted and love. Sounds simple enough, but we as women have become selfish by putting *our* wants and needs, before our man's. It's no wonder or surprise that he goes out and gets the things that he desires to have in one compatible complete companion – from somewhere else. Many times he has to find and utilize emotional pieces and contributions from different females just to have the total package of a total and complete woman/spouse/mate. Then we want to label a man as a dog because he goes out and seeks what he wants and needs from one woman-in multiple women. *Can your man get his complete women completely from you or does he have to piece together his emotional needs from multiple women. Can you get what you need and expect from your man or are your expectations unrealistic based on you and your issues or mindset?* Also where and how a man meets a woman may impact the type of emotional piece of his heart that she gets from him if any. I heard Pastor Tony Brazelton preach one time about a person's heart being an intimate place. Much like someone coming to your house and only being allowed in the general living spaces like the living room, dining room or family room, the heart is the most intimate place on your body. Usually unless someone is a close family member or friend they do to have access to your bedroom which is the most intimate place of your house. In a relationship a person's heart should be off limits until a relationship foundation is established.

Don't discount where or how you meet someone. If you recall the section where I state that the man should search for you then realize that the person who God may have for you may not be waiting for you in a fancy restaurant while he is driving his Mercedes Benz. He may actually be somewhere that you would least expect to meet him. Maybe he decided to commute and not drive his car that particular day and therefore he was standing at a bus stop; or maybe he was on his way to the Laundromat and just like you did, he *threw on something* to go there; ok maybe his hair isn't cut? Are your nails done? Get the point? Spending time with someone will confirm, verify or contradict what was portrayed in the beginning. The truth always comes out over time. How you met him may or may not be an indicator of who he really and truly is and how you meet him my dictate the path of the relationship. For example, if you meet in a club and he doesn't go to church, you can't expect to have a *Christian start* to your relationship. Now if you are a strong enough Christian and are trying to live a Christian life and then he may see and respect your beliefs and may even decide to go to church with you…Before I go any further let me pause right here for a moment. One other important point is that we as women cannot allow a man to give us *minimal* and get our *maximum*! Whenever I am dealing with a sales component of my business, I try to emphasize to those who will be spending money that they are making a minimum investment to get maximum exposure. This means that I try to show a client/investor that they are getting a great deal for the money that they are spending/investing…Honestly, it is a play on words; but it works to get and solidify the sale. A man should want to provide his woman with the opposite: a maximum investment for minimum exposure of what things look like especially to others. But in order to ensure that this is the case, we can't let a man give us just anything and we just accept anything. Nowhere did I say he had to spend a lot of money but it is an awesome thing for him to try (*wink*) and make an effort! It is ok for a man to express the magnitudes of his affection towards you. But be careful…balance is important.

At no point and time should the amount of money in which a man spends on you dictate his love or control over you. A man should want to give to and do for you because he cares about you and he is doing things from his heart's desires to and not out of obligation and/or expectation of getting something in return. And likewise so should we towards him. I love being in an *in love* friendly giving competition with the male whom I am involved, whereas we try and out give to one another love expressions (not who can give the better to show off). Essentially we love each other a great deal and we try and express the magnitude of our love through emotional and materialistic means. But at no time should money be a compensation for an emotional investment into the relationship from either a man or a woman.

Women act out and men act in. Most men are taught not to cry and/or to be limited in showing their emotions often called their soft or feminine side. We as women can be *cry-*

babies. Every woman that a man truly loves and gives his heart to continues to hold a piece of his heart-forever. We on the other hand can be *Indian givers* when we give our heart to someone. First we give it away too easy. Then later we either reduce the amount of the piece of our heart that we give to the person; take back the piece that we gave them, or abandon it and leave it there with them to spoil. (Side note: we cannot expect our ex(s) to put their life on hold and wait for us to come back. For me it's a hurtful thing sometimes to see a man from my past whom I really, truly loved involved or married to someone else, especially when I am involved with someone else and our relationship isn't working. The fact that it still hurts after a period of time shows me that a piece of my heart is still there with them until I call back my soul ties from them. I explain more on soul ties in Chapter 17).When we reduce the amount of space in our heart towards a man and/or leave it aka don't get closure from the emotional, spiritual, mental and/or physical ties, resentment and bitterness is able to grow in our hearts like mold. Our heart then hardens and could begin to change the way our outer appearance looks as well and cause us to stress out.

Are women spoiled-*YES*! Many of us have the desire to be *wined and dined* (me included). But our desires *NOW* may be causing our *LATERS* to be stagnating. Let's look at how much dinner and a movie cost. An average movie cost about $25 for two tickets and snacks. Dinner at a decent restaurant for you both can average around $100 (unless you decide to go on a fast-food restaurant candlelight dinner). Now, if a man takes you out twice per week that is about $250 per week. That's $1000 per month. That's $1000 that he could be investing into a business, paying bills, or investing his money so that a time can come when money isn't a predominate thought on your mind or something which you need to be overly concerned or stressed. But still spend it wisely. Instead of working on establishing a future, he has to spend money on you and other things that he has in life (e.g. bills, child support, etc.), and with the way that the economy has been, he may be barely keeping his head above water, and staying afloat financially. This is just something to keep in mind while selecting and negotiating outings, with our mate. I'm not saying that we should never be taken out anywhere *nice*. Let's keep the record straight, he can take you out to a nice place but he doesn't have to spend a lot of money. I would love for a guy to take me on a picnic in a park, whereas we eat and spend quality time. He can spend less money and be creative, which is not *cheesy* or a *cop out*, which could reveal more about him to me. I want a man who can intertwine his intimacy and genuinely caring about me, with his creativity, to make me happy while spiritually covering me.

SMALL THINGS NOW FOR BIGGER THINGS LATER- SIZE MATTERS!

By doing so, he may actually be able to buy me my chocolate - diamond ring without going into debt and sooner rather than later. Hopefully he is thinking the same way. However, since we don't share a brain our methods may be different. So we have to be mindful that our ways, thoughts, experiences etc. may not be the same as theirs.

Men and women, and people in general may originate from different backgrounds, experiences, teachings, geographical regions and more. Just as we may have been raised independently to cook, and clean for our man and do other *girly* things, he may have been raised to be independent, to work, and be a provider or he may have been taught to cook, clean, sew and be domestic.

First take time to learn your man's wants and needs. Then **MEET** or **EXCEED** them! If he likes home cooked meals then cook; a clean house-clean; massages-massage; etc. and do them well. Invest your interest in his goals and assist him, but don't try to edit or cancel his vision. It's ok to make suggestions that may help him especially if you have the experience and/or connections, but it is not ok to make alterations. Show him that you have his back and a genuine interest in your mind and that you are in his corner working with him. Make sure that he knows that you are his biggest fan and supporter.

Can you be your man's support system, special lady and best friend in the various aspects of his life to include his hobbies? If he likes watching sports join him and watch them with him and later he may watch a *girly* movie with you. However, don't smother him. Invest the time and welcome the opportunity to share in his hobbies, even if they include sports and video games. Welcome friendly competition with him also. Video games can be fun especially if he thinks that he is teaching you how to play…lol. Find the midpoint between spending quality time with him and smothering him by wanting all of his time and energy.

If your man is going out on a *guy's night* or if his boys come over, be a good girl around his boys but don't overdo it. Support your man's interaction with them but don't entice them by creating a situation. (Side note: Although you can't control anyone else's actions or behaviours, even if you wear baggy, unrevealing clothes his boys may try to pursue you because they can tell that you are a good catch. If he/they do try and make advances towards you resist the advances and don't fall for them. Is one slip up worth risking your entire relationship? Nope. More than likely your man is no longer going to want you because it will be extremely difficult for him to forgive you and move past an incident of infidelity- especially if it is with one of his boys). You don't have to be completely covered from head to toe with a turtle neck and knee hi socks but feel free to still look and feel good about yourself. A *trashy classy* outfit (like clothes that you feel and look good in like nicely fitting jeans and a tank top **WITH A BRA**) along with a nice non enticing demeanour or intentions is good but being too sexy can send the wrong messages to his boys and cause drama. In other words you may want to hold off wearing your booty shorts or transparent/short/tight/revealing clothes around his boys, even if they are at your home; but be comfortable. Wear what you would wear if your biological (not your play) brother was coming over.

As long as you do your part to show your man that you genuinely love and support him, and if he is confident in you, and assured that he has a chance at being mentally, spiritually, and emotionally stable – he aint going nowhere!

Chapter 14
Man Up

Women have expectations based on our upbringings, and past relationships. For example if we meet a guy who appears to be weaker than other men and/or the situations that we've had to endure, there is an underlined expectation that the new male has to supersede our past, and he has to try harder at being the *best* man for us. Although we may have visual and mental ideas of what manhood or being a man is, we can only create expectations but never definitions of a man, what he can be, or who he is.

There are several ideas and attributes which we as women may have associated with and use to describe or define a man being *a man*. These attributes, descriptions, definitions, and expectations may have come from us observing and learning from the men in our lives such as our fathers; grandfathers; uncles; brothers; male cousins; Godfathers; stepfathers; nephews; male pastors; deacons; ushers; co-workers; boyfriends; and husbands. Of course we may also have women in our lives like our mothers; aunts; sisters; ministers; grandmothers; cousins; deaconess; first ladies; co-workers or friends who have taught or suggested to us what and how a man should live, be and conduct himself. But the million dollar questions that we should ask ourselves is *how are the men in our lives interacting with the women in their lives whether she's their "significant other" or not. Are they respectful? Do they run through or "dog" women? Do they try to "score" with as many women as they can? Do they refer to or call women bitches, hoes, hores, jump offs, THOTS, sluts, or freaks?* Have you ever heard them talking to other males about *getting some ass?* Did you see any of them participating in acts of domestic violence, or abuse? What about them bragging about not taking care of their children? Having children with multiple women? Drinking excessive alcohol? Letting women take care of them? Placing more value on insignificant or materialistic things than the lady in their life? Have you overheard stories about males from other generations in their families, and how the men in your life may be continuing various traditions of other males in their lives? If this is all that you have been exposed to –when you tell a man to *man up* is it because you expect your mate to be opposite of what you see, or have seen? Or do you expect him to duplicate the type of *man* ideals which you have been exposed to and/or encountered? Maybe you have told yourself that because of the experiences that you have had in your life with males, you either want the same, similar or different…

Women can never tell a man to *man up*, because we have never been men. One day while my mom and I were sitting and having dinner at my mom's favourite restaurant Olive Garden, the song *Let a Woman Be a Woman and a Man Be a Man* by Dyke & The Blazers came on. We as women don't understand how to be a man or what men truly have to go through physically, emotionally and mentally to be who they are. Again, we cannot think like one – because we have never been and never will be one. And really we have to be mindful of what and where our expectations of a man came from. Another problem is that we have not learned to stay in our place or as I like to call it our lane, and let the man make the rules as it relates to us wanting a man to *be a man*. This may be one of the most difficult things a woman especially one who is independent can do. Hopefully, after reading the next few paragraphs, clarity will be made on what I mean.

When a man is in order – not *our order* but whereas his heart is after God and he is in good relationship with God, then he can love a woman. But instead of making sure that a man lives up to his *Godly standards,* we try different tactics to get him to be the man we want him to be. Many of us are single moms; divorcees; and/or career focused. Some of us are *Daddy's little girls;* while some of us wished that we had a relationship with our *sperm donors.* (Side note: I deemed my dad one because that is what he chose to be even after I made several attempts to build and establish a relationship with him. Out of three daughters he only choses to have a relationship with the one who is by his wife. She is the middle child and neither my baby sister or I have any type of relationship with our dad.)But whatever our modus operatus a man can be strong minded and still ignore our tactics and techniques. Regardless of how much we want to-he may not want to be the man we desire. We can't question his motives about ev-ver-ry thing. Our job is to help him; not to annoy him. Sometimes we just have to go with his flow, and be patient and have faith that he will make the right decision and not stir us in the wrong direction. More times than not he has a plan being downloaded in his mind by God-he just may not be able to share part or any of it with us right away. Don't try to teach him a lesson because he is being strategic.

A female can only teach a male but so much about being a male, and again her teachings are limited to the men who she has been exposed to either directly, through stories, books, television, movies, or other females. Again, we as women cannot think like a man because we have never been men, and vice-versa. No matter how much we temporarily or permanently alter our outward appearance, our insides will always be female. Does having a sex change surgery on a person's outer body change who a person is on the inside? Does it cause confusion? Does it really change who a person is? I personally have no idea or facts. Maybe someone else will answer that in their book.

Chapter 15
Bamboozled

The late Gerald Levert stated that he would *like to find the love he sings about in his Songs*. For me, music gives me memories and transitions me to other places in my mind – some good and some bad. Just because I am the author and can include this part – some of the songs that take me places are: *Before I Let You Go* by Blackstreet (reminds me of Daymon and the day he dropped me off at school the day before he left to go to the military)*; Love Won't Let Me Wait* by Luther Vandross (reminds me of my cousins Kirk and Lillian's wedding reception); *One Sweet Day* by Mariah Carey and Boyz II Men (reminds me of the time I sat crying and regretted having an abortion); *On Bended Knee by Boyz II Men* (reminds me of when I received my first marriage proposal from Maurice who used to sing Boyz II Men's songs to me frequently)*;* The Gospel Music songs *One Day at a Time; Blessed Assurance; and Come Thou Fount of Every Blessing* (and so many more by unknown writers-remind me of being over my Grandmother's house. My Grandmother Montrue is the one who taught me music from the beginning to include playing the piano – a lifelong skill, gift, and talent. *Come Thou Fount of Every Blessing* was her sister Yvonne's favourite song and I can still remember her sitting at Grandma's house singing or humming it as someone played it on the piano); *How Great Thou Art* (writer unknown-reminds of my Great Aunt Martha's house and the precious times I shared with her even when she sat at her desk and made me practice the piano over and over); and I hear my Mama's voice singing *Oh Lord How Excellent and A Change* (writers unknown). Music can take me to a happy or sad place. So…instead of listening to sad and depressing songs all the time, sometimes I have to turn up the volume on the stereo in my house or car and jam: Frankie Beverly and Maze (*Before I Let You Go*); Chuck Brown (Various songs); Pharrell Williams (*Happy*); *old skool* Hip Hop and of course uplifting good old and new Christian Music! It's time that some of you change the emotional musical tones in and of your life…how? You should be asking yourself that one – remember this book is for sharing the things in which I learned.

I have to admit that I am guilty of jamming to songs about being a happily single lady and to prove it I should throw my hands up. Beyoncé also performed with a group called Destiny's Child asking if a man could pay her bills, and she also declared that she is a survivor. In the later years she asks her man if she can pamper and cater to him. Yes, Beyoncé also put on the airwaves about us paying her bills, and we did just that by purchasing her albums. But now she appears to be happily married to rapper Jay-Z with a child named Blue Ivy. Oh, I cannot forget the song *Find Me a Man* (Tony Braxton); *Giving Myself Over To You* (Jennifer Hudson) and not being taken for granted because of the song *Superwoman* (Karyn White) also play in my mind and heart depending on the stage of romantic relationship that I am in with my significant other. In other words a happy heart and a happy mind equal songs with happy lyrics being played. However, if my feelings; heart and mind are unhappy, I tend to allow unhappy music to resonate out of my audio speakers. But this chapter isn't about my musical preferences or music; it's about our minds being influenced by people, places and things outside and around us. Although some influences can be beneficial-some can be detrimental.

Ladies we have been bamboozled by television, radio and films. We have allowed things around us to influence us and our relationships. Meaning that we allow what we watch, hear, see and taste to infiltrate our spiritual being and then it ultimately affects our outer self. I once heard someone say that "everything that looks good aint good for you." But if I could just take it one step further. "Everyone who looks happy in a relationship - may not really be." So if I had to combine the two – I would put it like this. *Don't ever compare your ideal relationship to what or how you see someone else's.* It may not be what it appears to be or depict how things really are within their relationship. For example, does an abuser walk around broadcasting and showcasing that he/she is an abuser? Although, the truth and signs can eventually surface and come out the answer is probably no. While I'm on this subject, this is also why it is important not to watch pornography. *Why? What does that have to do with anything?* I'm glad you asked. When you watch pornography you develop a somewhat unrealistic sexual fantasy of your mate. Yep, the guy on the video may *do some things* that you man just refuses to do. Hmm…maybe it's because your man respects you and the guy on the video is an actor and could be collecting a pay check. Besides do you really want your man to become a video porn star *giving it away* to different and random women? Or do you want your man to have wild sex with you instead of taking his time and making love to you? That's just something to think about? We can't allow what we see to dictate reality, and we must remember that our eyes and mind may be playing tricks on us. In other words, what we see or think is happening may or may not really be what is happening. The truth-is even if it takes a long time to do so, always comes to the forefront. Are you truly happy or putting forth an illusion to impress others? It is the job of the devil who is also called by different names to include *A Thief* to provide illusions and distractions by lying, killing and destroying. *The thief cometh not, but for to steal, and to kill, and to destroy: I am come that they might have life, and that they might have it more abundantly.* (John 10:10)

Chapter 16
You Dictate How They Treat You

Ladies, we set the standards of how a man treats us and if he should contemplate getting into a relationship with us. There is an old saying about giving a man the *milk without the cow* which defines and describes the justification, of why a man may not entertain thoughts of a committed and monogamous relationship with us. Why should he? He is getting all of the bottom line *benefits* without putting forth an effort of any sorts.

Before I go any further let me take a moment to take this *commercial break*. Here is a friendly reminder…just like a man wants someone to treat his mama; sister; daughter; aunt; cousin; grandmother; godmother; god sister; best friend etc. with respect and like gold – you are a female (with one or more of these titles) in someone's life. What makes any male in your life think that there is not someone, who is ready and willing to seriously hurt and/or kill someone, for disrespecting you- like he would, if another male did the females in his life; the same way he may have thought about and/or does or treats you? If you feel as though you are being disrespected, and if you are uncomfortable about the way that he is talking to or treating you then address it. Either he is going to conduct introspection on himself and make changes, or it is time for you to end the relationship.

Now back to the business (smile). When you allow a man to get your body without a commitment you may be considered a *jump off*, and not his *main* or *only girl.* Take a moment and ask yourself – *what do I have other than my body to offer him and encourage him to want to stay with me? What do you say? What do you do? How do you think? How do you act, to make him want to leave?* There must be some reason for him to truly want to be with you. He needs a reason better and more than because of your body because there are women everywhere. And based on what I have been hearing about the ratio of women to men- the choice is really theirs, but we have the option to accept their offer.

I often say that I can be selective when dating. The reality is that *I am* a female; and as long as I *am* a female, there is going to be a male who will try to engage with me – with or without a commitment. Not to mention that since I am made in the image of God *So God created man in his own image, in the image of God created he him; male and female created he them*. (Genesis 1:27) Men are like pennies whereas all pennies aren't pretty and shiny. Some are broken, dusty, chipped, rusty and upon further review foreign currency, and of no value to me. Get the point? I can find a penny or a man just about anywhere. Even without looking for it, the penny or the man just show up and seem to appear from out of nowhere.

A female's body has what a man's body needs and not just sexually. So why jump at the first man who shows me attention? Pause…I love myself and because I do I can appreciate the offers. However, I appreciate those guys who don't even try to have sex with me much more. I've had guys who have tried to camouflage their intentions which however still came out blatant, obvious and predictable. It's disheartening especially when God shows me a man's *true colours* about who he is before I even get around him, and yet I ignore and eventually fall for his game again. For example, I had met a guy and we talked briefly via online we believed that we had known each other from somewhere before but we couldn't figure out from where. Then he asked me to call him but instead I gave him my phone number and told him that he could call me when *he* was available to talk. That way the first move would be on him and his pursuit of me would begin. Well a few minutes later he called me but then indicated that he had to go into a meeting and would call me later. He texted me later and then eventually called me again. Throughout our phone conversation he just kept asking me could he *"come and cuddle with me*". I told him "*no*" and used every excuse that I could think of. Eventually I went out with him stupidly and although everything was telling me not to, he made me feel as though we were really going to have a future together. I mean, we had so much in common along with similar personalities and interest including music. Well we eventually ended up having sex and this guy who had called me consistently and would stay on the phone with me just about all night long until the sun came up – now was too busy with work and not feeling well enough (not because of me or anything sexually lol) to call. So I finally texted him (since he was too busy to talk) and said that it was over. I got an immediate response.

"Wow, I didn't see that coming but ok take care".

Really? It was as if he tried to flip things around on me. And for a moment I even began to feel bad for ending things without talking to him. But that guilt only lasted for a moment since I quickly remembered the events surrounding our five day relationship. Life definitely goes on and I am definitely his loss.

When a man has to invest time, money, energy, and mental stamina into you, he may be more willing to wait for a return on his investment. Don't let yourself be treated like a quick fix or foreign currency. Win the battle over yourself, and wait for the commitment. I have also learned that a man can place us in an emotional category based on how much a man has to *work for us.* Those categories are a *play sister* (a good friend); *a jump off* (just sex) or *his girl* (the type of woman that he wants to be in a relationship with). Based on how you conduct and/or carry yourself will determine which category he will place you in. Please see Chapter 23 for more information on categories that you may be put in if or once you have sex with a man.

I am a firm believer that you deserve whatever you tolerate. A man is going to treat you how you REQUIRE him to do so. When you carry yourself in a manner whether good or bad – then that is the same manner in which a man is going to treat you *good or bad*. One of the worst feelings that I have experienced is to be intimate with a man, and then feel like he made a conquest and got another notch under his belt. Especially, if I had initially set my mind and told him *no* in the beginning, and then allowed myself to become weak and ultimately change my *no* to a *yes*. Afterward, I feel dumb and have regrets. Then my regrets turn to anger and then resentment until I let the thought of the occurrence go by trying to forget that it ever happened. I know it's easier said than done. *However*, one of the best feelings is when a guy cares about and appreciates you. And does whatever he can to prove that he does. He doesn't just say or text it. But each and every interaction has pleasant memories for the most part. I know that a relationship is between two individual people and disagreements may arise. But the good days should outweigh the bad days of the relationship, especially, when a man can accept me for me regardless of my faults, failures, and imperfections. Around this type of man I can be myself with no mask, no makeup and he will desire me whether I have on sexy or *chill* clothes.

Now, I am not oblivious to the fact that our clothes do not dictate how a man should treat us, but it is how we act in those clothes which make the distinction of how he treats us as well as the appropriateness of the clothes. In other words are we wearing the wrong type of outfit at the wrong time and in the wrong place? For example, wearing sexy and enticing clothes at work, church or for a PTA meeting are not appropriate. *Do you stick out more or switch your butt extra? Do you make your boobs bounce? Do you wear a see through/transparent shirt and bra that can be seen?* A man wants other men to admire his lady from a far, and not be able to see all of her *hidden treasures* like her breast, butt and thighs. It's ok to show a modest amount of your body parts but stay conservative. (Reminder) Once married a women's body is only for her husband's pleasures (*The wife does not have authority over her own body but yields it to her husband. In the same way, the husband does not have authority over his own body but yields it to his wife.* Proverbs 7:4) and she should only want to entice and keep her husband intrigued. Whether dating or married a woman should not want to attract the attention of any and all man whom she encounters; but one special man.

Be sure to act like you want to be treated as good or better as he would want someone to treat *his* ladies. Encourage him to remember your value-assuming that you too know your value and worth. Don't decrease your value and cause your man to treat you less than what you should truly desire to be treated.

Chapter 17

Just Sex

When I spoke to several of my male friends about the subject of *just sex* they all agreed that men cannot be direct and upfront with a woman and say "all I want to do is to have sex with you" because it may mess up their chance of *scoring, getting some*, or having just sex with a female.

Have you ever thought to yourself or had a conversation with your girls that included this: *"Okay so I gave him "some [sex]" and he never called me back and/or his attitude changed! Now he wants to start acting funny! No more constant and/or random emails and his text have turned to maybe a "like" on a Facebook status. Seriously if all he wanted was sex then he should have just said that. Don't have me thinking that this "sexual encounter* [safe word]*" was going to lead to us being in a relationship and that I was going to be his "girl [spouse]"*. Ladies don't tell him that if all he wants is sex – then say all *"I want is sex"*! Let's be honest, that's not the reality that we really want to hear and/or ultimately face or be told by a man.

It hurts like hell when we are intimate with a man and then he acts as though he no longer wants us. I feel used and discarded and like he has officially played *me*. But not for long, because he then turns into a challenge to me. *What does he mean that he doesn't want me?* One way or another I'll get him? The rejection can sometimes feel unbearable and may be the underlying contribution to women having low self-esteem, depression, and a lack of confidence with a man. Or we can become emotionally blocked from men and begin to engage in sex with multiple partners sometimes within the same day or hours…But why are we as women so affected by sex? Well in the words of one of the best female rap groups Salt-n-Pepper *"Let's Talk About Sex"*.

Biblically – the Bible teaches us to not fornicate or have sex before or outside of being married, because there is an intertwining of our spirits which takes place. Emotionally it starts before a woman loses her virginity. Being a female, we should already know by now that physically a girl has a membrane which blocks the entrance of her vagina, called a hymen. When the hymen is broken due to penetration from a male penis, she is no longer a virgin. (*Side note: a girl's hymen can be broken from strenuous activities such as horseback riding, and high leg kicks. This does not mean that she is no longer a virgin because again she has not been penetrated by a male's penis).* We never forget the first sexual encounter that we had or the day that we lose our virginity. First because it hurts; and second it causes us to have strange and unfamiliar feelings. Our body has now been *invaded* and our spirit has now been connected with someone else's spirit. A human being is made up of an outer casing called our body; a mind to control our body; and a soul which connects us to God. Sex is a spiritual act between two people which causes our bodies to engage in physical activity and our spirits to intertwine. According to scientist, we as women are walking chemistry labs who physically release a non-hazardous chemical from our body. In my opinion, scientists have tried to give a human/scientific explanation to a spiritual action. *Ok so you are the "go hard" take charge and assertive woman of the new millennium and it's all about you "getting yours"* I got it…But when it comes to sex you can't even carry things that way. Why? Because no matter how hard we try to categorize and mentally condition ourselves to think about it as just sex- it can never be *just sex.*

When a man and woman have sex there is a chemical called oxytocin (ox-e-tox-in) which is released and helps bond a relationship. It creates an emotional bond and should be associated with the ability to maintain a healthy interpersonal and psychological bond and boundaries with the other person –

another person. This is especially true when oxytocin is released during an orgasm. Although, it has other functions like assisting with mother/infant bonding, the more you release this chemical to other people (plural) the greater the bonds (plural). In other words, the more sex that you have and release this chemical to *one person*-the greater your bond with that *one person*. However, if you release it to *multiple people* you are bonded with each and every one of *those people*. Vasopressin is another chemical hormone which assists in forming the bond of a monogamous relationship because it plays an important role in social behavior; sexual motivation and pair bonding; and maternal responses to stress. Lastly, Endorphins not only play the role as the body's natural pain killers, but they also aide in the bonding between two people, by providing a general sense of wellbeing to include feeling compassion, soothed; peaceful; and secure.

Ok so if we keep sharing and releasing hormones we may end up feeling empty. This makes it hard to separate our physical and emotional feelings from our sexual partner.

Now I do agree that men should place their desired intentions in earlier rather than later conversations with us, because early conversations can truly reveal a lot about a person, if we listen and take everything that they are saying into consideration. Be sure to watch and listen, for the indicators from him that all he may want is to have sex but he disguised them behind false imagery. Then we can decide if we want to choose to take and chance the possibility of being hurt, or if we can save some time from going through and experiencing unnecessary drama.

I used to think that it was blatant disrespect if I spent time with a guy and then the next day and/or days after I didn't hear from him. I was pissed! *Am I the only one who has said and/or felt like that? How could you spend time with me and have what I thought was a magnificent time and then not call me the next day. Were you pretending to be interested in me for that amount of time or…No excuse! Then one day out of the blue you just call me like nothing abnormal has happened to pick up where we left off? Are you serious? You have some nerve.*

In the past I probably would have called a guy and cussed him out for not calling me after we had sex. But I had to learn that I'm not his wife until we say *I do* and a man not calling could be a sign of immaturity or disrespect. You will know the difference based on the conversations you two had prior to, and surrounding the time that you spent with him. Follow your gut feeling and the vibes. *Is he arrogant? Does he talk about how he has no desire to be committed, or to get married? Does he act like he's God's gift to the world because he has obtained some nice material things?* (I'm not hating) *What has previous encounters proven?* As far as immaturity, his mind may have just not grasped the connection between intimacy and emotions. Especially if he, himself has had struggles with being insecure. He may be committed and loyal, but not ready to perform all of the *Mister* duties that occur during a marriage. If I am not in a relationship already (or close to it) that also means that I am not obligated to perform all of the *Mrs.'* duties either. Oh, and this is especially true if he is still legally married to someone else! Even if he is separated and possibly on the verge of a divorce– he is still someone else's husband. Although, I am a firm believer that there are three sides to every story-his side; her side and the truth; and being unmarried, we as single people have to totally stay out of his marital issues. I've been married so I understand that married life and single life are totally different.

Single life is about an individual, whereas a marriage is about two individuals becoming one and no longer seeing life for just them individually but collectively. (On a side note: You want to have and maintain a happy marriage but you keep watching shows like "Maury" and "Divorce Court". Stop polluting your mind and spirit and *feed* them positivity. I'm not dissing those shows and have to admit that I watch them too some times. I just try to limit my mind and spirits exposure to them. Because of the audio and visual seeds of negativity, that I may begin to plant in my relationship may produce a harvest (result) that I do not want. Additionally, if you are not spiritually mature completely avoid TV shows, night clubs, etc. which contain negativity because of the negative impact that they may have on you).

We can't be the judge and/or jury as to why his marriage with her is not working out. He may like and be interested in you but he can't be ready to be with you. If he is going through the process of ending a marriage, you have to first do one of the most unselfish things in our being to do – push him to reconcile. In God's site, he and his wife are a part of a threefold cord that cannot be easily broken. *Two are better than one; because they have a good reward for their labour.10 For if they fall, the one will lift up his fellow: but woe to him that is alone when he falleth; for he hath not another to help him up. Again, if two lie together, then they have heat: but how can one be warm alone? And if one prevail against him, two shall withstand him; and a threefold cord is not quickly broken.* (Ecclesiastes 4:9-12). They have made a covenant to God, and one another; and you are not the third part of that chord. If we don't encourage him to at least try and reconcile WITH HER, then he could end up hating and/or resenting us for possibly playing a part in his regret about losing his marriage. I believe that a man is tormented most during the time of a marriage ending because in his spirit he knows that God hates divorce and that he is going to have to give an account to God as to why his marriage ended. A woman is emotionally torn but she will be emotional all her life, so this is just another *adjustment* for her. It's almost as if she is expected to be even more emotionally damaged because of the divorce. If a man seems to be indecisive about what he wants to do about his decision about what to do about his previous relationship/marriage don't force him to choose because in doing so his choice may not be you. Then if he does in fact end the marriage and after the ink is dry on the divorce papers, you have to still give him time to breathe, and relearn himself. Don't allow him to jump from one relationship to another.

Give him time to heal, be delivered from the hurt and pain of his failed marriage, and gather his composure, so he can give himself over to you fully. His emotions as well as his heart need time to heal. Guys are attracted to the woman who has something to offer him other than just her body for a relationship. But a woman with only her body to offer a man is a temporary fix of what he really hopes to successfully have-a relationship with his wife.

Chapter 18
Hide and Seek God

It is possible that if we go to church with the wrong intentions- that we may get the wrong results. Point blank, your husband may not be at church, so stop going to church to find him. Go to church to find God - not a spouse. One of the reasons is because the church is like a hospital, whereas people who are emotionally, spiritually, mentally and *physically sick* go to get healed. Take it from me first handed, especially since I have personally had several people prophes-lie about my spouse attending the same church as me, and I went to church looking around for a man instead of looking for a relationship with God. And each and every time that I did, my searching got me nowhere. Nope! No boyfriend; no relationship; and no marriage. But this methodology is not limited to just looking for a man in church-but anywhere we choose to look to include clubs; our jobs; the grocery store; the mall; the car wash and gas station. He may not be who we are expecting or anticipating him to be either.

Just because a man looks good and he has potential because he attends church, doesn't mean that he is ready to be your husband; even if he does know how to pray, shout and speak in tongues. And on the "flip side", just because you have been in church *all of your life*, doesn't mean that you are ready to be a wife, even if you do know how to pray; shout; and speak in tongues.

There are some people who come to church with mask on to hide their true identity, of not being *delivered* after being demonically possessed by evil spirits and with evil intentions. This means that they can imitate what they should be doing during certain parts of the program in church, but they do it without the power of God, and the Holy Ghost! They are faking it and not making it! The bible even warns us *"Let no man deceive you with vain words: for because of these things cometh the wrath of God upon the children of disobedience.* (Ephesians 5:6 KJV) I like how it is translated in this version: *don't let yourselves get taken in by religious smooth talk. God gets furious with people who are full of religious sales talk but want nothing to do with him. Don't even hang around people like that."* (Ephesians 5:6 NIV) And yet despite our knowledge of church protocol, none of us are perfect and we all still have various types of issues. No one is perfect but God. *And Jesus said unto him, Why callest thou me good? There is none good but one, that is, God.* (Mark 10:18)

Similar to the issues that we as women may struggle with daily, men struggle with insecurity, lust, abuse, *baby mama drama*, alcoholism, and more. When I go to church I seek to escape from those things and look to hide under the *shadow of the almighty* (Psalms 91), meaning I look to God to relieve these burdens from me according to God's plan, and will for my life. While I am seeking God's refuge, only the man who God ordained to find me as his wife-will find me.

Whether or not in a church building, club, a grocery store etc. the Bible says *that he who finds a wife finds a good thing* (Proverbs 18:22). It doesn't say *when a woman finds a man she wants, she should go out and pursue him.* It is better for a man to choose and decide that he wants you, than for you to choose and decide that you want him first. One of the worse things that we can do as woman is to stroke a man's ego by pursuing him. Ultimately, if he wants you he will do whatever he can to get and work hard to keep you-if he *does* chose you. In some countries and religions, it is customary for a man to pay a woman's family money called a dowry in order to marry her. The more he wants her the more he will pay to her family to be eligible to marry his potential and desired mate. Whether in money; time or energy, a man should still somehow try and invest in his pursuit of a mate. Even something as simple as a phone call, email or old school handwritten letter to the woman he is pursuing is an investment.

A man should call a woman first. Even if he offers to give you his phone number, decline and give him yours. Pace the communication but don't expect him to call the same day. A man who seems too eager and persistent seems *pressed* and the question you should ask yourself is why? *Is this a sign of emotional issues*? I want a man to call me in a few days after he gets my phone number. Make me wait and wonder. *Why?* Because I want him to be a man who is confident in himself and who he is; and I want to be an addition to who he is. I know you are probably saying that that sounds like I am playing a game with him. Actually I am not. I am seeing how desperate that he is, and how pure his motives are. And when he calls I want to see where the conversation is going to go. Is he going to recall special and memorable moments that we discussed from when we met; or is his *when am I coming to see yous* merely about him getting sex? (Side note: For those of you who do not feel comfortable giving out your phone number, I use Google Voice services. This free service screens my calls and that way if I do not have an interest in continuing an interaction with a man, or any one for that matter; I can easily not answer their calls or block them. Eventually, and hopefully sooner rather than later, if I'm not interested he will stop calling. But that's after he has called the first time and I give him the benefit of the doubt of making an attempt at getting to know him. Also with his calling first he may show me that he appreciates the fact that he gets to pursue me and that I am not rushing home to call him, immediately after we met. Now a days the first points of contact may be via *Facebook.com; Tagged.com; LinkedIn.com; Hi-5; BlackPlanet.com, Twitter.com; Instagram.com; GooglePlus.com; Pinterest*; *Myspace.com;* or others. The same rules still apply-let a man pursue you!

You are the *drink and not the chaser,* and a man should work to earn your heart. In an alcoholic drink, the *drink* is the most important part of the *mix*, not the juice, water, soda or even ice that it is mixed with. Whether the alcohol is mixed with something else or by itself it is the most important part of the beverage and can be drunk alone. We as women have to look at ourselves as being an intricate part of the relationship. *Do you love yourself? Are you secure enough in who you are that you can be alone (the drink) and still be that secure and love yourself the same or more once you are mixed (in a relationship)?* (Side note: I used this example because it gives the best illustration. I'm not using it to encourage anyone to go and experiment and/or drink alcohol. A guy told me that he was the drink and not the chaser one time, and it stuck with (even though he was incorrect in using it). Anyway, there are some men who you are not supposed to be involved in a relationship with. Even if he does choose you – if you are unequally yoked, incompatible and/or God has already told you *NO!* – Respectfully decline. A former co-worker of mine once told me to guard my heart, and I took this to mean for me not to just give it to any man who appears interested in getting my heart.

In order to do that you will have to use discernment, and not your desire to be *wifey* to offset your own issues. Please, please, please don't be so desperate that you accept a spouse in your life, who is not going to love and respect you, and who feels that he; his wants; and needs are more important than you, and yours. If I meet a guy and he appears "*pressed*" I am immediately turned off.

I was coming home from work one day and this guy invited himself to my house and told me that I was going to be cooking him dinner. He even told me how long it was going to take to clean up my house. First, how did he know what my house looked like on the inside? Second seriously this dude is tripping! Needless to say that was our first and only conversation other than later when I waved and greeted him from a distance. Now to some females, his antics would have appeared flattering. But to me, he was downright pushy, and rude. I mean how was he trying to invite himself to my house and then make all the rules? He was definitely not the man for me, and I was okay with that.

Oh, while I am nearing this issue, if you are not married, and things do not work out between you and your spouse, don't be so devastated by the breakup that you miss the breakthrough. Although I don't condone divorce, there are some exceptions like abuse and adultery, which grant a pass to get one. Someone may have to move out the way for the person whom God has for you to be able to get to you. We can become consumed and distracted, while we are wallowing and feeling sorry for ourselves, and *let ourselves go.* Our potential mate could be scouting and searching for us, but isn't attracted to our outer appearance; or lack of self-esteem and/or emotional damage. Does he really need to pass us by because we look a mess mentally, and physically? We may be able to suppress being *jacked up* mentally and emotionally…but for how long? (For more on this, please see *Chapter 19: Bottle Up the Glow*). If you do maintain your inner and outer beauty, do not try and force a relationship either; especially if you just got out of one.

A few guys have told me on numerous occasions that *you are a female, so you will always be able to get a man* (there were some other choice words, which I omitted from their statement due to vulgarity). That is true and also means that I can be selective in the type of man that I want. But the bottom line is that a man may try to rush us into a relationship with him- especially if he too recognizes that we are good women. Or as I like to call myself -*a prize.* If after a few conversations, I recognize that a man who is trying to pursue me is an admitted *slick talker* who *double talks;* or only trying to have sex; or appears *pressed;* or if his conversation is dull, absent and doesn't keep my attention-he has to go! No more conversation is needed, because I am no longer interested. And worse, if he lies to me once, my thoughts and considerations of letting him become more than a friend decrease. If he begins to reveal that he is a habitual liar, and *slick talker* or that he is not what I desire and doesn't line up to the type of man God wants me to be with, at first sign he is *dismissed.* That way he can move out of the way of the man-my future king who is trying to find me! *(Side note: as I am writing this part I just thought about a few more people who I am going to have to dismiss.)*

Chapter 19
Bottle up the Glow

Are you making yourself available to be approached? When you walk do you walk with your head up or do you look like you are ashamed and lack confidence by walking around looking at the ground and afraid to make eye contact with someone? Are you having loud and meaningless conversations while you are on the phone or in person and sound obnoxious, ignorant, ghetto or as if you are seeking attention? Are you acting as your own *man* repellent?

Keeping up my outer appearance always makes me feel good, especially, when my hair and/or outfit look *hot*. I personally love looking and feeling good from top (my hair) to bottom (outfit and shoes); inside (emotions) and out (physical appearance). I want to make sure that they complement one another to create a *total package*.

I can remember in one of my dating attempts, a few days after the guy and I agreed to be in a committed relationship, different people in my various environments said that I was *glowing* and that they can *see the glow*. They complimented me on my skin tone, hair, makeup and clothes. Stop! I know what you are probably thinking and the answer is *No!* I was not pregnant. Subconsciously, what I felt on the inside was being reflected on the outside of me. I felt happy and excited about my new found *love prospect* and I guess my body was definitely reflecting what my heart and mind was contemplating. In fact after I smiled and got a *warm and tingly* feeling when I thought about him; I relived in my mind things he had said; the way he looked at me with his gorgeous hazel eyes; and I could even feel him touching me-even though he was nowhere near me. I was motivated to get up for work in the morning just so I could count down the hours until I would be able to get back home and await his visit.

Until *it* happened...two weeks later.

My dream was to have a household whereas *as for me and my house, we will serve the Lord. (And if it seem evil unto you to serve the LORD, choose you this day whom ye will serve; whether the gods which your fathers served that were on the other side of the flood, or the gods of the Amorites, in whose land ye dwell: but as for me and my house, we will serve the LORD. Joshua 24:15)* He offered to come and go to church with me but I declined because I was searching for a new church home and didn't want to be responsible for him being misled, with us visiting the wrong church. I wanted him to be lead to follow Jesus Christ! On this particular Saturday during a very hot summer we were looking for refuge from a major thunderstorm the night before which caused my house to not have gas and electric. As we planned to find the best cooling spots, which ended us on my front stoop and we began talking about religion. Now I don't mind having discussions and *agreeing to disagree*, but keep it respectful to all those involved in the discussions. He totally disrespected my Christian beliefs by calling all Christians liars and hypocrites and wrong. I was pissed and told him that our relationship was over and he left my house. I'm sorry but God and following Jesus Christ has brought me too far in life for me to allow anyone to disrespect Christianity, as a religion or Jesus Christ as my Lord and Saviour. He is going to be held accountable at God's judgment because he had heard the truth before about who God is and the way to fully have access to God through His son Jesus Christ (*John 14:6 NIV Jesus answered, "I am the way and the truth and the life. No one comes to the Father except through me*). It was only my job and my purpose for being in his life was to tell him the truth based on what the word of God says, not based on my opinion.

Over the next few days, I missed him very much. For a brief moment, I even thought about sacrificing my beliefs and standards to reconcile with him. Every day, I hoped we would run into each other and unfortunately one day we did. And once again he totally disrespected or *carried* me. He had the nerve to tell me point blank, that the plans that we had made for our future together were put on hold because *he needed some space and time*. He kept reiterating that he did not want to have to look forward to constantly dealing with drama. I tried to reassure him that that wouldn't keep happening. And I honestly almost totally lost myself. *WAIT A MINUTE! Hold up! I'm the drink not the chaser and the prize*. He was totally trying to play me for a fool and I was about to let him!?!

God had already showed me that this man was not the man for me and his actions confirmed this revelation. *If he loved me, then he would not disrespect or hurt me on purpose.* So, I quickly gathered my composure and walked him to the door and said, *"I'm glad I found this out now"*.

After he left I thought about the entire encounter and all that had happened. *Maybe I should make another attempt at being with him. Maybe I messed up. Oh well, I guess I'm going to be alone again.* Yep, all of these questions and thoughts did come to mind. But I quickly decided that instead of me being devastated and falling into a *funk*, depression or being sad and bitter about losing him – I was going to be twice as happy now as I was with him- *without him.* I was going to reproduce and make more of *the glow and maintain it*! Now I am going to illuminate happiness so that when I get complimented on the glow, it will not be because of a man being in my life or something that a man has done to or for me. But because *Greater is He that is in me than in the world* (1 John 4:4). Oh, in case you are wondering, the glow comes from being anointed and having God in my life. It is just the outward evidence of what is on the inside of me. God is dwelling on the inside of me and He is shining brightly in my life. Yep, I had to stop and take a praise break right here.

There are lyrics to a popular song which say *"this joy that I have the world didn't give it to me."* As the song is sung other verses include the word "joy" being changed to peace, love, etc. I can now add another verse: *"this glow that I have the world or a man didn't give it to me; since the world or a man didn't give it –a man nor the world can take it away"*. If you need help with finding your glow-find God and/or rededicate your life to Him. It's ok if your glow starts out as a small flame. Eventually if you keep allowing it to glow it will grow into the flame that you desire. If you are suffering from loneliness, depression, anxiety, anger, bitterness, hurt, pain or anything else, then you will have to empty out these feelings first. *Neither do men put new wine into old bottles: else the bottles break, and the wine runneth out, and the bottles perish: but they put new wine into new bottles, and both are preserved.* (Matthew 9:17). Please get yourself together so that you can bottle up the glow.

XV.

Rest, Divine, Grace, New Direction:

What is He REALLY Saying?

Chapter 20
Decoded

I had met a guy on Facebook.com or Tagged.com (I can't remember) and we had been *seeing* each other on a quick and temporary basis. After about a month or two he began to fade off until eventually he stopped calling me and vice versa-I stopped calling him. Actually and although I backed off because I realized that we were unequally yoked due to our religious beliefs, I still tried to work with him for an "us".

Then there was another guy who I had resided with during my *house hopping days* Rondelle. We reconnected on yet another popular networking website, and we wanted to see each other in person after all of those years of being separated. I was curious as to whether or not those same feelings were still present after all of this time. We had both been in marriages, which ended in divorces, and he also now had two children. After conversing briefly, one day he picked me up and I rode with him back to his house, where I stayed the night. Needless to say, I didn't get a call or any other contact from him until he wanted to *hang out* again. Although this time around we didn't have a committed relationship, I started seeing a similar pattern as before developed by him. Whenever he needed to borrow money, or just got out of a relationship that didn't work, he called me *just to see how I am doing.* He even called to let me know that he had invited himself over and was in route to my house one time to meet his son. I told him that I was unavailable and I stood firm in my decision. Once I caught wind of his tactics, I think he was a little surprised that when he started coming over, he wasn't allowed to go any farther than my eat in kitchen, which was right at my front door. He tried extremely hard. He even had said that he was going to get me a cell phone and pay the bill, in an effort *to butter me up* to use me but it never happened. I just got fed up with the entire small talk, which always seemed to lead back to him *stopping by*. Now, after that one time after we *rekindled* I never suggested any other intimacy except an occasional hug (definitely not a kiss since he had absolutely no skills). He still tried. He would offer to work on my car without charging me, and do other favours.

However, the *no charge* car maintenance seemed to cost me meals, and gas money for him and his kids. There were even some times when he indirectly and directly asked me to borrow a couple of dollars. WAIT! You're probably saying *didn't he work on your car for free?* My response would be that I only asked for my car to be fixed if he called me- and remember he only called to try and get money or sex. Eventually, I had learned his *codes of conduct.*

Just like we have to allow a man time to learn our codes of conduct, we have to take time to learn theirs. There are certain *trigger* words that men use to *fish* (excuse the pun) to see where our mindset is, and if our words are on the same track as theirs. Are we willing to accept the bait and satisfy their sexual desires, or do we remain steadfast, and disobedient to *their* subpoenas.

A man's words and actions may not add up. You should listen to his words, but carefully store them in a file cabinet in your mind. Also, watch his actions because his actions may have to catch up to his words. In other words he may be saying some good stuff and you may doubt its legitimacy-but later he may be able to show you better than he tells you the proof. His actions will either validate or void the truth. Just as we dangle physical bait to get a man, they use their *words* to *bait* us. This is why it is so important for us to love and value ourselves. *Beloved, believe not every spirit, but try the spirits whether they are of God: because many false prophets are gone out into the world.* (1 John 4:1) That way our discernment is in full gear and he can differentiate between "*true words*" and phony ones. He may give false truths at the start of your relationship to impress you. In time the truth if different from what he told you will come out. You see the thing about a person who tells lies is that they have to work hard at maintain the truth. They have to remember what they already told you and build on it. With the truth, there is nothing to remember and no matter what or when the truth does come out it will be forthcoming; easy; and consistent. (Side note: Talking too much about ourselves can definitely turn a man off especially if he is not very talkative. Personally I don't like a man who talks more than I do because I feel that he is both self-centred and focused primarily on himself; or trying too hard to convince me and him of something. What room does he have in is life for me or in some cases-the truth? So in an effort to practice what I teach I try to shut up and be a good listener. However, I must say that in my defense and due to my background in media broadcasting, I do tend to try and avoid gaps of silence. But I do cherish *"golden silence"*. I feel that a man can actually tell me more in the way that he looks at me or with his kind gestures that he shows toward me rather than the things that he says to me. Plus if I listen and take mental note of what a man is saying, I can verify and/or contradict it later. Once you spend time getting to know your male mate you will learn that he may express his feelings in various forms. For example, he may be upset, frustrated or stressed, and instead of displaying weakness, he may actually lash out and display these emotions through anger. Instead of fuelling his anger, give him some time to gather his composure. If he genuinely loves you he will soften up. He may not even realize that he is displaying his emotions this way. Be understanding but don't be a door mat. If you really know your male mate-which again comes from spending time with him and getting to know him, you will learn not to take his emotionally displays personally, and to be understanding. He may not mad at you but at whatever situation he is facing. Let him cool off, and *get his mind right*. He will appreciate you for still being able to literally love the hell out of him, and accepting his emotional flaw. Even if he hangs up the phone on you or doesn't talk to you it is ok. Let him work through his issues. I have learned to make an agreement with a spouse whom I'm trying to create and maintain a meaningful relationship and that is that we can agree to disagree, and we are not going to always like each other. But in the end unless we both agree to end our relationship, the bad times are not going to cause us to break up. We are both two separate human beings with feelings and emotions, willing to fight for our relationship to work. We will allow for the good days to outweigh the bad days, and we understand that not all days will be good and/or happy.

Ok so let's get back to the *meat and potatoes* of this chapter. This next part is not for married women because once you are married your husband cannot deny you, and you cannot deny him of sexual pleasures. (On a side note: you should never go to be angry and not speaking because that will allow the devil to speak to you and the anger will fester, settle and root. The Bible says *Be ye angry but sin not. Let not the sun go down upon your wrath. Neither give place to the devil.* (Ephesians 4:26-27) But single ladies please pay attention.

Sometimes men will use different verbal and nonverbal tactics to explore females and the limits/boundaries that we will allow them to go. Some of the verbal tactics that men use tend to be extremely chivalrous. However, they can have a totally different meaning than expected. Do any of these sound familiar? *What's up with you? Let's hang out. I just called to say hi? I just called to see what you are doing. Can I come and see you? When are you coming to see me?*

Men (the ones who aren't trying to be platonic friends) may use any, almost or all of these inquiries to mean *I'm trying to see if you are available tonight, for my sexual pleasures.* And you may see that they are the statements that are attempts to have sex with you and are just that-sexual advances. Why? Because they typically are a prelude to what can be considered a negative response, if you decline. They include: *I'm going to call you back; let me hit you back; let me put my phone on the charger; why you be fakin'? Or send me some pictures.* Again, do any of these sound familiar? My hope and prayer is that you learn to discern the difference between *booty calls* and genuine calls of interest. Remember his words and actions may not line up; even though talking is a verb and an action word.

As far as the weight of man's actions towards me, they speak a lot louder than his words. If a man wants to be with me no matter how shy he is how much of a lack of *game* that he has, he will show me that he wants more than just sex from me. He will invest time, energy, and money into what he values. If the only time that he calls you is during *booty call* hours (although not exclusive to this hours but typically 12 am-4 am), or the conversation always leads to *in person* intimate visits then he may only want to have sex with you. And if you have already *given him some* and he only wants to have uncommitted sex then he is not your man, and you are like *coochie bank*. What is a *coochie bank?* You are a female and so you should already know this but just in case you don't... When you go into a bank, there are various transactions that can be conducted: a deposit, a withdrawal, a transfer, or balance check. Don't allow him to be with you to make sexual withdrawals, deposits and/or transfers. Make him *check his balance,* between intimacy, and in a relationship with you.

Single women-do you really want your body to be used up because you have been with so many different men before you get a chance to give the gift of your body to your husband? There are so many sexually transmitted diseases in addition to the possibility of you having a kid(s) by a *random* man who isn't your husband. Save your body, mind, heart and life. WAIT! And gradually work on being celibate until you are married. Love yourself more than just enjoying the temporary fix, of uncommitted sexual pleasures. Only time will tell, whether or not the *situation* that you are in with a man has relationship potential; or if the time you are spending is just so that he can get to have sex with you. I had met this guy one time and ironically he never had money, time or energy to come and see me especially after I told him that I don't allow strange men in my house. But one night after I sent him some "special pictures" all of a sudden he wanted to come over. I wasn't angry, because actually I tested his motives and intentions to see if he was a *wolf in sheep's clothing* (*Beware of false prophets, which come to you in sheep's clothing, but inwardly they are ravening wolves*) (Matthew 7:15) and he probably failed the test. He proved that his intentions weren't to establish a relationship with me, but to get to have sex with me.

Sometimes it's hard to decipher between a man's words and action because they can be deceiving. He may still spend time in person with you and/or call and talk to you on the phone. He may even feel comfortable enough to share his visions, goals, and hypothetical *what if's* about life events. But it is important for you to guard your heart, and practice effective communication with him, because effective communication produces effective results. Truly know where you stand, so that there will be no misunderstandings of the expected outcome of you friendship and/or relationship. Don't make the mistake of trying to read between the lines of his statements and verbiage. For example, if he says *I don't want to lead you on* he may truly mean *I don't want to lead you on.* His mind may have already positioned you in your place in his heart. Conversely, you may have caused yourself to be categorized and/or misjudged due to your own actions and decisions as discussed in previous chapters, as they relate to him.

In the past, I have been guilty of purposely ignoring what I hear from a man, and what he is saying. In my mind, I had already decided what I wanted to really hear from him regularly and what I wanted it to translate to. This caused me to have superficial hopes and expectations of relationship outcomes, and ultimately experience a lot of disappointments. Bouncing back from these types of disappointments can be hard especially when you *put all of your eggs in one basket.* Meaning that you no longer entertain or consider a relationship with any other male prospective mates; but focus on one particular male.

The bottom line is that you have to wait and listen to whom God said should be the person allowed to pursue you. For me to have a man who will not just love me but be *in love* with me is worth the wait.

Chapter 21
Mr. Telephone Man

Many of us have heard the lyrics to the popular r/b group New Edition's song *Mr. Telephone Man* and I think that there are times in my relationships whereas I have wished that I could have called a telephone repair man to make sure that my phone was working properly. I used to think that it was blatant disrespect if I spent time with a guy and then the next day and/or days after I didn't hear from him especially if we had sex. I was pissed! *How could you spend time with me and have what I thought was a magnificent time, and then not calls me the next day, for a few days or weeks or longer. Were you pretending to be interested in me for that amount of time or...NO EXCUSE!* Then one day out of the blue he would call me like nothing abnormal has happened and to pick up where we left off or send me a text saying *"hey lady"* or *"what's up with you"* or my favourite *"how are you"*? *Are you serious*? He has some nerve! In the past I probably would have called him back and cussed him out but I had to learn that I'm not wifey until we say I do-I can't. (Side note: although a man may be committed and loyal he may not ready to perform all of the Mr. duties in a marriage. That also means that we are not obligated to perform all of the Mrs. duties either. This includes calling on a constant or consistent basis, especially if no titles or descriptions have been placed on what you two are doing).

The question that must be asked of us is when did we become a doctor and require our man to have check-ups and check-ins on his every move? Yes, I know because of the connections that we have with him we miss him like crazy when he is not around. On one side I believe that if you are in, or trying to establish a committed relationship and/or marriage, then as a means of establishing trust, there should be no lingering questions. But if you are not his wife and you have just begun dating you don't have to know his every move, and he doesn't have to know yours. Now I know that in the beginning of me meeting someone who I would potentially date we would spend many hours on the phone during those initial phone calls. I would be tired as I don't know what the next day especially, if our calls lasted until the sun came up. But I didn't mind because the conversation was good and I was interested in him. The first conversations can truly reveal a lot and after some time, is an essential foundation for everything else for the relationship.

Another thing that we have to look at is that every day is training day. I often joke that Proverbs 22:6 says to *train up a man in the way he should go and when he is older he will not depart*-instead of *Train up a child in the way he should go: and when he is old, he will not depart from it.… (Guys it's just a joke I don't always think that men are childish even when they do spend hours playing video games)*. When training or teaching know that every man is similar but not the same. Just because one man acted a certain way in a previous relationship with you, said certain things to you whether the words used were right or wrong, doesn't mean all the other men you encounter will do, say or act the same.

Not calling the next day does not mean that he doesn't care or is not thinking about you. Maybe he was truly busy, not feeling well and/or tired. Maybe he has not had that responsibility before, or ever; or he may have actually forgotten. If you don't hear anything from him after a week, or a few days then maybe you are just *the jump off* and not his *girl*. This may seem childish but I have a waiting period. If a man doesn't call me-I don't call him. When he finally does call me he has had time to miss me –or at least he makes it appear that way. Eventually he'll either continue not calling or he will try harder to call or contact me more. More times than not, it has worked and a man has rededicated his commitment to me. Now, wait you probably just said that I am playing games with him about the phone calls. I'm not really. I'm actually allowing him to express himself, take the time to realize that he misses me and how important that I am to him and that he misses me. For *some* reason men tend to prefer to be the chaser rather than be chased…

Chapter 22
Leave the Honey Alone

I couldn't understand or comprehend a period of time whereas I was truly completely single yet I was only attracting married and/or involved men, and you know that each and every one of them gave me a sob story or *"woe is me story"*? The truth is that we as women have sob stories too, whether or not we want to admit that that is what they are when we give an emotional story to someone to invoke more emotions. In trying to be transparent I'll share one of mine which is not totally just my sob story…keep reading and you will understand.

I have always loved Kyle…But he doesn't trust me enough to be in a relationship with him anymore. However, he will still have sex with me (if I allowed him to), *and is always willing to do so. When I was married he comforted me. Once my marriage began to fall apart, I needed him for companionship and friendship and he was the man that I needed and during that time the man I wanted.* Two days before he got married he asked me to meet with him and have sex with him. Deep down, I believe that he wanted me to change his mind about getting married because he realized that he was truly marrying someone else other than me. Although there are very few things in my life that I regret, I didn't go and meet with him. Also, I had already tried to talk him out of it, and he ignored me and went through with marrying her. Years later he moved out of state and found me where he always seems to find me via my email. He even offered me the opportunity to have him fly me out to Florida, Las Vegas and Texas at his expense for weekend excursions which now I am glad that I declined them all. I know…Yes it was a hard NO! (no pun intended). One day I received two calls from his wife, after she hacked into his Yahoo email account and saw that he and I had been corresponding and sending each other pictures.

I intentionally hung up on her the first time and then when she called right back; I hit the ignore call button on my phone to send her to my voicemail. When she left a message she made threats and I could have had phone harassment charges filed against her because of the threats that she left on my voicemail. They included her *'being the wrong bitch to f&*k with'* and that she would sue Kyle and me. After I listened to her message, I called him and warned him that he was going to have hell to pay when he got home because she had found out about our conversations. Our communication briefly came to a halt and he waited some time but then he emailed me again. This time the conversation was even more intense, and this time he had me under the impression that he was truly miserable and closer than ever, to leaving his wife and that he and I would be together-finally. He even asked me to have a baby with him. And he had even planned a trip to come to Maryland and visit with me the following March near my birthday.

"I owe you that", he said.

Although my emotions were going crazy, I truly wanted to believe that he was coming back to me and our relationship, and going to be my man. However, I quickly realized that he was unsure, and therefore I convinced him that he really needed to stay and work on his marriage with his wife.

"I don't think you should contact me anymore. Stay and focus on your marriage, " I requested of him.

"Are you sure that that is what you want to do, " he responded.

"No, but I have to," I responded.

"I'm going to ask you again, are you sure that that is what you want". He responded as if he were trying to get me to change my mind.

I struggled for a while and then I answered again, *"Yes that is what I want. Contact me once the ink dries on your divorce papers".*

For one final time he responded,

"If that is what you really want then I'll do it."

You should already know that that was not his final correspondence. He sent me a text message almost two months later for my birthday...and then later with the same scenario of him being tired of his wife and told me more of her issues and how he wanted to leave her to be with me but it was followed by all of the reasons as to why he couldn't leave her. For example, he didn't want to risk not seeing his daughter and eventually because she was pregnant. Also because they could not afford to live separate due to financial hardships. I still encouraged him to stay with her in their marriage and work it out. But the more I encouraged him the more he seemed to show an interest in having a relationship with me. Although, this time it was more obvious that he was a little closer to getting tired of being married to her, his heart still wasn't ready to completely end the marriage. Later I still received occasional emails and text telling me how much he loved and missed me. And again I still encouraged him to stop being stubborn, go and make love to his wife and rebuild their marriage. He insisted that he didn't want her and was still in the marriage, house and with her for the kids' sake. Mind you they had like five children-two together and three which she had from a previous marriage. The entire situation with Kyle was starting to get insane.

A general definition of insanity is doing the same thing, the same way and expecting a different response. So after years of not asking a potential mate certain questions, and being disappointed by false hopes, I did start asking them some questions up front but still anticipated different results, until I truly learned.

These are a few questions that I'm bold enough to ask when I meet a guy: *are you married? You gotta girl? Who do you live with? How many kids you got? How old are you?* and *do you go to church?* These are just some of the preliminary answers that I need to know before our conversation goes any further and a man gets my phone number. I want to know if a man qualifies and meets my standards. This also helps me to see if this potential spouse he may be disrespectful to anyone who may be involved in this situation.

Every one of us should have established standards, qualifications and preferences. For example, I personally prefer to not to date a man with more than two to three children, he has to be Christian and with a job; his age can be no more than fifteen years older or four years younger than me, and he has have his own place of residence. Although, the guys I meet often don't meet all of these wishes, these are just my basic core preferences.

The point is that some of us have allowed ourselves to be *one of them,* instead of his main and only lady. Honestly, I used to be susceptible to settling for and sharing a man-just like some of you. It didn't matter. I dated involved men whether they were married or not. In fact, one of the things which drew me to my *ex-husband* was the challenge of knowing that he already had a girl living with him. *Who was she*? In my mind and at that time *obviously* she was not woman enough to keep him; or the woman for him to be with in a relationship-right? I mean she may have lived with him but he was interested in and pursuing me. *WRONG*! She was the woman she was; he was the man he was, and I was who I was. We all had issues. After I was reintroduced to my value and worth, I learned that even if a man is separated (and possibly on the verge of a divorce) he is still someone else's husband. Also, when I see a potential mate I do a scan and zoom right in on his hands. *Is there a wedding band or light ring mark around his ring finger on his left hand?* Some men don't wear their rings or wear them on the wrong finger/hand. I check *both* hands. If I see a ring the thought or potential of any type of relationship vanishes. If no ring is present I *deep* dive by asking him questions and try to see if he will admit to being married, or being involved in a relationship with another woman in any capacity. If he can lie about his relationship with her then I'm sure that he could lie about he and I's relationship if he wanted or needed to. I would prefer for a man to tell me his relationship situation and/or status up front, and let me at least have the option of how I would like to proceed. *May I have the choice of whether or not I would like to still deal with you or to leave you alone?* At least give me the option first before you decide for me by lying. Once you have lied to me the decision of me not dealing with you has already been made-by you; solely because you lied to me. A man should also do a "spoken for scan" of a woman for indicators as to whether or not she has a significant other.

Some of us wear a *Keep Away Ring* to keep a man from trying to pursue us for whatever reason. I tend to wear one regularly, just because I'd rather stay focused on my projects, goals, visions, and dreams instead of being distracted by a man with drama and issues. But does my *Keep Away Ring* keep away my good guy? The guy who has respect for another man's place already secured and established in a relationship. That possibly may be the case. But hey, I have to do what I have to do to make sure that my mind and heart stay on track and that I am successful and living in God's will for my life. A respectful man won't intentionally disrespect a couple in a relationship. Instead he will respect the boundaries of your relationship. He won't try to sway you to have an affair with him by courting you and/or trying to get you to have sex with him. We have to take that same approach about another woman's man –especially when she has the title and role of being his wife.

Regardless of what he tells you about the situation, we cannot be the judge and/or jury as to why his marriage with her is not working. If and when they physically separate, even though he may think that he may be ready to be with you do not engage in a relationship with and/or have sex with him. If a man is going through the process of ending a marriage, we have to first do one of the most unselfish things in our being to do – push him to reconcile with his spouse, If we don't encourage him to do so, then he could end up hating and resenting us for playing a part in his regret about losing his marriage. Just like just about every other thing in life, getting into and getting out of a relationship is a process. Further along in this chapter I define relationships so please keep reading. Think about it we have a process for getting dressed; brushing our teeth; driving our car; even our body has several processes which it goes through to properly operate and function. If he seems to be indecisive about what he wants to do about his decision about his current situation with his previous relationship or marriage then don't force him to make a decision. In doing so, just know that his choice may **not** be you.

Now he if does in fact end his marriage or relationship with another woman, to include the ink *being* dry on the divorce papers, and him thinking that he is ready by appearing to be over the hurt and the pain of the break up, he still needs time to breath, and relearn himself. Allow him to go through the entire process of grieving and healing. It is very important and in the long run very beneficial to you and the success of your possible and future relationship with him.

Here are the stages that I have observed and experienced, which are similar to a person grieving someone who dies:

1. hurt
2. disbelief

3. anger
4. acceptance

Hurt: Do not allow him to jump from being in one relationship to another. Give him time to heal, and gather his composure, so he can fully give himself over to you if a relationship with you is in his future. **Disbelief:** Right after a relationship he may be in a grey area of his emotions. He is trying to evaluate which emotions he should be feeling and how he should experience them. Remember a lot of men are taught to suppress their feelings. **Anger:** He may even feel devastated and lost because a woman whom he may have been involved with may have intentionally hurt him. Now on that note, the Bible says *Be not deceived; God is not mocked: for whatsoever a man soweth, that shall he also reap.* (Galatians 6:7). I have heard this same verse and its definition used in other cultures and labelled as karma. It simply means that whatever you put out in the spiritual atmosphere –good or bad, is what you are going to get back from the spiritual atmosphere-good or bad. If you treat people badly then people will treat you badly. For example, let's say that you always conspire to get someone in trouble at work and ultimately fired, be prepared to have someone conspire to get you in trouble and ultimately fired. So if he cheats on his girl with you then expect him to cheat on you with another girl. With that in mind –why do we think that he is going to leave his main girl – his good girl for us? **Acceptance:** To the male whom we are pursuing, we may appear desperate and *easy*. Will you really give and do anything to get him? If that is the case a man may come, spend time and even money on and with you, but you aren't quality enough for him to stay with you and establish or build a relationship. And if he does by chance enter into a relationship, after you get him, what do you have that is so good that he will want to stay with you? Ask yourself why would he *want* to be with a woman like you? Reality check-does he really want you or were you convenient while his girl was unavailable while at work/church/school/traveling etc.? You believe he really does want you right? Ok…what does he want from you? Every relationship opportunity is a gamble and the reality is that there is a 50/50 chance that it will or will not work out. Are you willing or desperate enough to take the chance or risk to find out? Or is being single the best thing for you right now? I'm not saying that this is going to be your final marital state, but can you honestly and seriously say that you are ready for a relationship? Are you being pressured by your friends and family to hurry up and get involved in a relationship, get married or have children? I personally had to learn that it is ok for my "biological clock" to be on snooze instead of continuously ticking.

In (Ecclesiastes 3:1) of the bible it states *To everything there is a season, and a time to every purpose under the heaven: A time to be born, and a time to die; a time to plant, and a time to pluck up that which is planted; A time to kill, and a time to heal; a time to break down, and a time to build up; A time to weep, and a time to laugh; a time to mourn, and a time to dance; A time to cast away stones, and a time to gather stones together; a time to embrace, and a time to refrain from embracing; A time to get, and a time to lose; a time to keep, and a time to cast away; A time to rend, and a time to sew; a time to keep silence, and a time to speak; A time to love, and a time to hate; a time of war, and a time of peace.* We and our relationship statuses have seasons. Sometimes we will be a hot commodity or meet and be courted by a lot of potential mates. But we have to be careful to sift through for the one who meets our needs and who has the most matches to our list of desired qualities in a mate. Oh! You don't have a list? Don't worry I have got you covered. Please see the back of this book under my section entitled *"Extras to Help You Further Answer Why You Are Still Single"* for a list that you can use as well as other resources. Even though it may be rare that we find a man who has every quality on our list, it's good to have at least a starting point. Our list of ideal qualities should include desires, expectations, and qualities. This list could be effective in starting and/or creating a conversation with your prospective mate. However, it should not serve as a script for you and him. Be honest and upfront. This man could be the one you enter into and develop a relationship with. But conversely, don't assume that you already know what his response is going to be. With all that being said, just know that there may also be times when you may not meet or be pursued by anyone. Are you ok with staying home or being alone or not being in a relationship? Or are you settling and accepting a man's minimal efforts for trying to establish a relationship with you? If you have been involved with a male for years and living on broken hopes of a future with him-then it is time to seriously think about and evaluate what is occurring between the two of you.

Think about and truly listen to the number of mounting excuses that you keep getting from him about not being able to be in a relationship with you. If he truly wanted to be with you, and there weren't any "legalities" or commitments involved with him being with someone else – he could commit to and be with you. Bottom line is that a man is not going to leave his *sure thang/comfort blanket* for a desperate, unqualified female who doesn't love or respect herself. A sane and *normal* man in a committed relationship truly wants a complete relationship with his current mate. However, she is not fulfilling his needs in some capacity; she is doing contrary to what this book instructs or he just has that many issues of his own and can't commit to one female. He may be very sweet and convincing, charming etc. but there is an old saying that *you attract more bees with honey than with vinegar.* If he runs to you every time she does something that he doesn't like; challenges him to be better, or doesn't spend enough time with him – stop him from coming to you. Do not allow yourself to be his *backup plan*s. You are a treasure and not someone's trash. Therefore, don't allow someone to treat you as trash, but as a treasure. Are you happy being a back burner?

Now here is one of the few times that being the back burner is ok. When I am cooking on a stove I prefer to first use the front burners on it. The burners on the back side of the stove are used for things which need to cook longer or to place empty pots while I utilize the front burners. In other words if you are content with being a back burner, are you going to be used to have something placed in or on you while you simmer and slowly develop or as a place to position emptiness and not being used until needed or as a secondary choice? Is he placing you there to slowly develop a functional and strong relationship or is he placing you there (like the burners on the back of the stove sitting there waiting and available) as a *just there in the event that you are needed?*

You are not less of a person nor is your worth any less than his main girl is or anyone else unless you make yourself that way. I had to grasp that concept too myself, because I used to avidly shop on Craigslist.com and search for cheap *hand me downs* or things that people no longer wanted and/or that they considered trash. I had a poverty state of mind and placed limits on my financial abilities. However, one day *Eureka*, I found it-my value and worth. I decided that I was worthy of getting new items. *Why settle for someone else's trash all the time instead of occasionally and when I found a great deal or something like an antique or rare find?*

I'm not saying that the man's other woman is trash. If a man who is in any type of romantic relationship with anyone other than you, you need to tell him as one of my male friends Mike told me ***LEAVE THE HONEY ALONE!*** If you are already involved with an already involved man, try to put a stop to it and if he still actively pursues you, cut all ties. If and when he calls you on the phone-don't answer. Pick up without saying anything and then hang up the phone or sit it down off the hook. Eventually if you are steadfast, unmovable; consistent (like the Bible says in *1ˢᵗ Corinthians 15:58 Therefore, my beloved brethren, be steadfast, unmovable, always abounding in the work of the Lord, since you know that your labour is not in vain in the Lord)* he'll get the point and hopefully he will leave *your honey* alone. You should want to begin to be a sour vinegar-like taste to him. That is perfectly fine! If that is what's needed to get your sanity back –then be that! Instead of being *wishy washy* be strong enough to say: *No. That's N-O PERIOD. It's too much to deal with you and wait for you to decide when you want to deal with me. Sweetie there is a man out there who wants me, my time and EVERYTHING else that I have to offer. And yes I knew what I was getting into when all of this started but Honey I want better and more, and you can't provide that so there is need for me to stay on standby waiting for you or to go through these motions. I've become celibate.* (Side note: you may want to really try being celibate).

One of the worst things that I feel that a man can do is ask for me to share his time, attention and heart with someone other than God, his family and himself. In other words, if he claims to like and/or love me, I should be his only mate and spouse. Asking me to *"wait in the wing"* to decide if he wants her cake or mine too should not be an option or an issue. It's just not a fair request to ask me to be the woman who makes him happy and fulfils his needs without any strings or commitments or effort on his part to be solely with me.

(Side note: Sometimes when you are dealing with a man who is in an awkward stage of in between commitment and trying to break up knowing and being involved less is more so that you won't get entangled in what is going on during the break up. This is also true if he is involved in illegal activities. Trust me if police get involved the more you don't know the better off and you are less accountable that you are to the case. Anyway, it should be easier for you to decide not to be involved with that man. But it all is based on how much he has established and earned your trust and how much you are willing to sacrifice for him).

Until a cheating man is delivered from cheating, he is always going to be a cheater even if he promises that he won't. If he cheated on her with you, more than likely he is going to cheat on YOU –with another HER! Erase his phone number out of your phone and ignore his emails, text messages, and social network post. Cut off all means of communication-even if does send a person or a kite!

I read online one day *that burning bridges are good because they keep us from going back to where we should have never been in the first place. Huh? LaDonna what are you saying?* I'm saying that there are some people, places and things that we have come across in our lives, which we should have never allowed to enter into it. We ignored and/or did not know or recognize God's voice telling us *NO!* So we did whatever we were grown *enough* to do, and went where we were grown enough to go. But look where we ended up.

Many of the situations that we may have gotten pushed in to may have gotten us more dirt thrown on us than we were willing to be dug out of and from. Meaning we may have had to deal with unnecessary issues; drama; phone calls; name calling and more. In finalizing and ceasing all communication with someone if you are having difficulty than ask yourself these questions: *Why am I burning the bridge? Is it a bridge that I may need to cross again at a later time? Can he stay on my team as a resource and not necessarily my mate? Or do I need to sever all ties immediately and just leave the honey alone?*

Chapter 23
Just a Friend

So you meet a guy and he seems like the perfect man. It's been a few weeks and things seem to be headed in the right direction of a long term relationship. What is the first thing that we do in this modern age of technology? Yep…go and update our status on Facebook. And then we enjoy all of the "congratulations", "likes" and well wishes. But then a few weeks later we have to change our status to "single" or "*it's complicated*", because our quick relationship start has come to an abrupt stop or ended due to issues. The point and the lesson that we should learn is that we need to wait to update our Facebook and other social media statuses. Waiting to update online and real life statuses is a must. Especially, when you are working on trying to persuade a man to marry you. If he has not mentioned a ring or marriage, do not start planning the wedding. (On a side note: if a man discusses marriage during sex it doesn't count. He may not be serious and could just be caught up in the moment and feelings of the sexual intimacy. Wait until he discusses it while he is *sexually sober* do not take the conversation about marriage seriously. Notice I said let him bring it up. As I mentioned in earlier chapters, don't allow your biological clock and/or pressures from family and society dictate the marital timing of your relationship. However, do not allow a man to have all of the benefits of a marriage without the actual marriage. *But among you there must not be even a hint of sexual immorality, or of any kind of impurity, or of greed, because these are improper for God's holy people.* (Ephesians 5:3) He may get comfortable and see no need to have an *official marriage.* I am truly convinced that men tend to confuse themselves emotionally at times, about the emotional difference between "*officially married*" and "*just friends*". Then in turn they confuse us, but then they can't understand why we act kah-ray-zee when a man says to us that *we are friends.* We as women tend to invest so much of ourselves in to a potential mate and to feel like the time spent was in vain and wasted is a hurtful feeling.

I am always curious when I meet a man about his motives for wanting to interact with me, and what type of interaction is he expecting to have with me? *(*Side note: this is definitely the case now that I have books out. I am still humble but I have noticed that some men want to be with me or have tried to have sex with me just so they can have me as a notch under their belt, and have bragging rights about having sex with me. *Why*? Because I am confident in myself plus we may have had a conversation and he may have already confirmed that I am one of if not the best type of female that he has met. I know I may be a step up from some (or a lot) of females they have had or are surrounded by. I'm just me-a challenge not a conquest.*)* Anyway, some types of relationship interactions and definitions that a man may try to use to define his interaction with us are to be platonic; to be friends with benefits; and or an intimate relationship. Let me take a moment to define each one.

A ***Platonic Relationship*** means that within the relationship between him and me, that there will be no sex. Yes, it is possible to have a committed, platonic relationship even between a male and a female, and not have sex. I have several male platonic friends, whom I have been friends with for long periods of times even decades. Like Bryant, Sean and Wayne, whom I have known each for a minimum of ten years each. However, it does take discipline and self-control. The desire to have sex may arise but you BOTH have to fight the temptation, and avoid convenient opportunities. Opportunities like: being alone, and with enough privacy to establish a sexual atmosphere and mood.

A ***Friend With Benefits*** relationship is where there is no expectation of a committed relationship and yet there is a respect and care for one another with the bonus of having sex.

Before I continue with the next category and while we are defining- let's talk a moment about the different levels of sexual intimacy as I define them.

The first is ***Casual Sex*** you may call it *just freaking* (to use a safe word). There are no strings, no commitments, and no attachments and no expectation or intention of a relationship or commitment. This is not truly acceptable to me or desired, and can very hurtful especially if practiced under unequal expectations and/or motives. This is also where the category of *one night stands* falls.

The second category is ***Sex***. Now you may say *"isn't that all levels"*? Based on my definitions – NO! Take my hand and walk with me through these definitions a little farther. Sex is the level when the *friends with benefits* mode of operating comes into play. You may *hang out* and be *cool*. But neither of the parties is interested in or wants to be in a relationship with the other and maybe dates someone else. This is kind of an interior *"I'm horny"* and want to have sex with someone that I already know and trust.

The third category is ***Making Sex***, and is the result of one or neither party being ready to have any type of a commitment. The difference between *making sex* and *sex* is the ability and willingness to be in a relationship. The individuals may genuinely care about one another and ***have love*** for each other, but they are ***not in love*** with each other. This is also the stage where a couple who was in a past relationship is able to still have sexual encounters; but again without the *"danger"* of being in a committed relationship.

Lastly, but the category of these being defined by me and that I value as my ultimate desire is ***Making Love***. This is when I love someone and I am in love with them; and we both care about each other's wants, needs and desires. At this stage, there is an intimate and passionate physical expression of the love, and our feelings are mutual and satisfying. This stage is beautiful and fulfilling. It is also the level of intimacy which is supposed to be shared and expressed in a marriage. Although

I've only been genuinely in love a few times, I have learned that his level is rewarding and fulfilling because it satisfies my human and Godly spiritual desires from a relationship. It's full of love and affection and the male and I are on one accord and in agreement as it pertains to our relationship.

A man's actions and verbiage towards you will truly define and identify which level you have been placed on by him. What I have discovered is that the actions of a man really do speak about the same if not more as his words. In other words he may say that you are *just friends,* and use it as a defense mechanism to protect his heart due to his previous hurts because he may be trying to get a feel for you and what you are about. Or because although the *"relationship"* may be appearing to be moving forward-he may be trying to slow down the pace it to truly get to know you?

A sad reality is that when we find a man who by our standards is good-we sometimes set our sights on keeping that man how we think he should be kept. Instead we have to take time to keep his interest and his heart. They hold more importance than being intimate with him. I learned that when a man says friendship it's just that - *friendship.* We as women don't want to hear the words *just friends* because we live on hopes and fantasies, and many times we are horny or allow our biological clocks to time our relationship desires. To avoid any misunderstandings, talk to your man *a lot* in the beginning stages to begin to learn what role you are going to play in a potential relationship with him. Ask questions and be open to a different answer than what you may or may not expect to hear, because relationships do not have any scripts to map out what should be said; nor do they have obvious answers. However we know that hurtful words, name calling and insults should never be intentionally or consistently said. Be careful that you carefully convey your messages and get your point across with respect. If you want effective communication and results, as well as get a potentially satisfying answer from your man, don't talk *at him* talk *to him.* You are not his mother –you are supposed to be his partner. Even if he does act immature he is a grown man. Again, he is not your child. If he was adult enough to be your "man" love and respect him as just that-your equal – your partner-your man – your covering.

(Side Note: *Why* do we say that we are settling down once we get into a relationship or marriage? We need to start saying that we are satisfied now. What should be satisfied is our wants; needs; and desires; and they are because we have been found by a man who wants to do as he has been instructed by God. This man is going to want to honour, love and respect us which is as God instructed him to do: *Husbands, love your wives, even as Christ also loved the church, and gave himself for it;* (Ephesians 5:25). The only time that we should use *settled* is if we have decided that we are not worthy of a quality man or a man who is solely committed to us, and we are taking or settling for the left overs from that man who treats us less than the best way that we deserve. So once again you haven't *settled down* you are *satisfied now.*)

However, to also avoid further misunderstandings and/or potential embarrassment, don't miss his signs. He may be ready to settle down and you may or may not be his choice. If you aren't then move on.

If you are- don't blow it.

XVI.

Love:

How to Lose Him

Chapter 24
Second Time Around

Have you ever walked down a mall passage way with a guy, and noticed that he took one glimpse at someone and then another. Notice I said at someone not at something? Something awesome did not catch his attention while he was window shopping and he wasn't look at the window displays either. Instead the girl walking nearby with her booty, breast, and legs exposed by wearing figure revealing clothes, or a body revealing outfit has caught his attention and caused him to be intrigued. *Yes girl, he did do a double take right in front of you!*

I have also been driving and/or riding in a car with a guy in my car, and noticed him taking more than one look at a female standing outside at the bus stop or driving in the car beside us. Me being me, I made the comment *she's phat* (in this cause it is an acronym for *pretty hot and tempting*) and it caught him off guard. Stop…wait…no I'm not a lesbian, or anything like that. It was simply my way of letting him know that I saw him taking more than one look at her, and that I was on the verge of feeling disrespected. The guy would sometimes become defensive and then sometime in the next few minutes or so, we would be engaged in an argument, and for what? *If the look was as innocent as he said that it was, then he wouldn't be mad or defensive right?* No-I'm not being insecure. How would he react if it was me who was looking at another man and taking multiple looks? I truly felt that way until I matured to the point of mentally asking myself *"am I really acting jealous over her?*

Eureka! Finally one day I had an epitome! Who is he in the car or walking with – me! Not her or them – me! God gave he and I eyes and just because he looks it doesn't mean that he's going to touch, even if he does take a second look. He may appreciate the beauty of a woman. Honestly, even I have to admit that she or her outfit looks good (no homo). When I think about it, I may have taken multiples looks too at her shoes, outfit etc. In fact, I have noticed that women take more looks, make more mental notes and even sometimes make comments whether good or bad, about other females. Sometimes we look at a female's body shape in clothes and wish that our body shape did or did not look like that. Come on ladies keep it real up front and honest! Sometimes the comments that we make are secret desires for ourselves, in terms of weight loss/gain; body shape; designer label etc. Even if we do not want to admit it – we may want ourselves to look that way as well. *Oh, so you don't want to admit it? Ok then why are you going to the gym and working out? Why are you trying to find a brand name or major label at the thrift store?* Yep think about it. Anyway, let's get back to the point before I spend way too much time on this part. He may have been taking another look imagining you in that outfit and contemplating buying it for you. Here's an easy way to remind yourself not to jump the gun" and get upset with your man just because he uses his eyes to look at another women once, twice or however many times. If you are woman who is secure in yourself, then it doesn't matter where he gets his appetite as long as he comes home to eat. This simply means that whether he looks at one woman twenty times or twenty women a gazillion times, as long as he is just looking - so what. He's coming home to you. Besides don't you look and sometimes multiple times at a man who is *fine,* good looking, and handsome? Do you go and sleep with him after you have looked at him? Even though in our mind you may think about it and want to; hopefully you don't. Now I try my best to make sure that a man that I am in a relationship with should have no permanent reason to be thinking about and/or fantasizing about perusing anything with the woman who he has taken a notice of. His look should be just that - a look. A man should not disrespect his lady and stare nor should he dwell on a dominating or lingering thought in his mind about her. We as women are more inconspicuous when we take our "*looks*" and we may be able to just look at another man and mentally move on. Men are more sexual beings who think about sex every seven seconds. So although he shouldn't try to hold on to his thoughts of another woman – the reality is that her image may linger in his mind a little longer than we would like for it to.

(On a side note: If you are the girl that is being "*looked at*" balance your ego and flattery scale. In other words, please don't let it go to your head and you become *big headed or conceited* because of the interest of a man. It should not ultimately define your behaviour causing you to be egotistical. Also along those same lines, please do not begin the "*ho stroll*". You know where you *switch your butt* extra hard; or even stick your butt out further, stick out your tongue; or in any other way entice him. That is not the way to get a man to want anything but sex from you. He may be attracted to you and that could be your way to "bait" him in…just for sex. If you want more…do less. You have already caught his attention for one reason or another. Now give him fair opportunity to get to know the inner you – past the outer you or your appearance. That is if he is not in a relationship).

However, all flirting is not harmless and can cause a lot of unnecessary drama between you and the lady in his life; or between he and you due to your feelings of getting hurt by him. A look does not necessarily equate to a man wanting you. He could just genuinely notice you and keep on with his life.

A lot of if not most men were raised to look at and admire the beauty of a woman by other men "teaching them the game". Yes guys, I have heard conversations of older men advising and instructing younger males on, and how to do this. But ladies have you ever seen a man who is *F-I-N-E?* Maybe he has a shapely muscular built body, even if his face isn't all that cute? Let's just be honest for a moment. Have you happened to see a man who *just-looks- good* because he has the body shape and attractive face that we want and deserve?

When we are with our girls we may take obvious multiple looks, and may even include an "hmm", and a high five, within our "*womanhood*" circle. We can even give codes verbally and non-verbally and interpret each other's messages. When we are out with a male significant other in our life, we are much more discreet with our looks, and are more prone to think –rather than express, our thoughts for other men. The thought may float from one side of our brain to the other, and drift away. But do I or have I looked-yes. I've even noticed that a male out with me may notice my look, and look in the same direction. Well me being me-once I notice him looking, and to also avoid any drama, I change the subject and redirect my male significant other's attention to something else. Who wants to deal with the drama of him accusing and making sarcastic remarks? Would he observing me observe another man-give him the *green* light to look at another female, or to do more with her than just look? If he did I truly believe that I would know!

How? I am a firm believer that we as women have women's intuition, *which means that we will (many times) just know some things. Are you like me and wonder if a man can tell in any ways other than sometimes physically when we've been intimate with another man?* Lol. I say they can't sometimes tell based on several factors. May I be transparent? Of course I can since I am the one writing this book. Our vagina is a muscle which contracts and there are several ways to make a muscle contract and become *tight*. And that is all that I am going to say about that. (On a side note: Ladies, there must have been something or some reason that you had an encounter with another male. *Were you lonely or feeling ignored by your man? Did he no longer seem to care about you? Did you try to flip the script and hurt him because he cheated on you and you wanted revenge? Are you assuming that your man had an affair or do you realistically know for sure?*

I often question the fact that some men do not show an interest in me until I ignore them? *Why does it take me not accepting your calls/emails/text/Facebook message or wall post, before you decide that you are interested? Why is it possible for me to tell you off and give you a piece of my mind and you act like it is an aphrodisiac? Then why is it that I finally do correspond back and you act as if you had won the battle?* Is it an ego *thang*, or does a man feel threatened when I am no longer easily accessible and at his beckoned command? Does he feel that he can sit my heart on a shelf or in a vault or safe until he wants to be bothered with it or as a *just in case* his relationship doesn't work with someone else?

In either case much like the United States legal system is supposed to be, it's hard to win a court case with little or no evidence of doing *whatever*. Before you accuse your man of infidelity there are certain steps that you should take to solidify the proof in the conversation, that you are about to have with him.

The first is to NOT listen to outside influences or opinions about you, your man, and your relationship. Especially, if you are married-a single person cannot give you advice about a marriage-PERIOD. They do not have the experience of being married. If a person has never had experience in something and they have never personally experienced – then they can only give an opinion but no advice. The person who is acting as your source could be scheming to get your man, or a man scheming to get in your pants, by acting like he genuinely cares and is a *shoulder for you to cry on. Wake up*! He could be preying on your vulnerability. And this may include people who use *"churchy"* lingo or false prophecies as well! Remember God does everything in decency and in order. If there is confusion it's probably the devil making an attack on you.

Second, make sure that what your mind sees-is really what your eyes see. Don't let your mind play tricks on you. Make sure, that your issues from past or current relationships with people outside of the relationship with you, and *your man* are not inducing imaginary thoughts. For example, if an *outside* man flirts with or tries to pursue you, and your entertain it; subconsciously your man's cheating could mentally be your own. Also do not let people plant bad mental seed in to your mind by saying or showing you things like pictures or actions about or from another man to you. This could cause your mind to wander and open up curiosities about another man, leading to your cheating on your current man or ending your relationship. And yes watching strippers and pornography counts because you can also develop unrealistic expectations from your spouse. Oh and here is a friendly reminder – strippers and porn stars are actors creating an illusion and fantasy. In other words, much of what they do and how they perform is not even real. Their job is to entertain whoever chooses to watch them perform.

Third, have a non-accusatory conversion with your man, and voice your concerns. Again, **talk _to_ him** not at him! If you yell at him, he may tune you out, and become unwilling to listen, and you'll blow your opportunity. Have a calm and successful conversation, where you voice your thoughts and feelings, but also listen to your man. Again, I say don't just hear what he is saying-listen. Give out your feelings and receive his response-even if you don't agree with it or it wasn't what you anticipated. Remember, as I mentioned previously, there is no official script; manual; or guidelines for any relationship. Success in and with a relationship comes with trying and erring; and learning from the good <u>and</u> bad experiences. Hopefully, he will reassure you, and you two can move forward pass this issue. If he gets mad and defensive, then further conversation needs to be had. Just like I mentioned in Chapter 20, don't allow your doubts to be harboured inside your mind and fester. Especially if you are having this discussion before you go to bed. *Why let it carry over to another day?* Deal with it now!

Fourth, if you begin to see a change in him and the *signs* become obvious and blatant then it's time to end the relationship. These signs may or may not tell a true, factual, complete or accurate story of what may or may not be happening. Be sure to look at the entire picture. Make sure that your mind has not painted an imaginary science fiction type of picture of the situation. Don't let your mind be the cause of your heart's defeat. I personally hate feeling defeated and that I've lost at something, especially if I invested a lot of time energy and tried hard at winning. If what you are seeing is what you are really getting then you can be oblivious to the signs.   Some of the signs and behaviour changes are cutting off his cell phone around you when normally he has it on and has even told you to answer it before, but now you are no longer permitted to answer it; his interactions with you change to include but not limited to no longer having sex with you; speaking disrespectfully to you; and his calls becoming sporadic or obsolete. His heart and attention is somewhere else. If you truly love him – IT IS GOING TO HURT. But in time your heart will heal if you allow your heart to heal from the relationship. Do not allow a man with whom you are in a bad relationship with to be allowed to be a blessing blocker of the relationship that you are supposed to have – with someone else.

Those same signs may have also began to create and foster the feelings or lack of feelings towards him that you feel in your inner being, especially when you have given the relationship time to matriculate and they may or may not be true about what is happening within your situation. However, unless you know for sure that he is cheating or has cheated on you; make sure that you have given him a fair opportunity to love you before you totally dismiss him, unless there are other obvious issues like drug abuse, domestic violence etc.

Again, and I can't stress this enough- if the blatant evidence is not there, focus more so on allowing positivity to seep into your relationship. Even within the United States mathematical system a positive number multiplied by another positive number equals a positive number. But when a negative number is multiplied by another positive number the sum equals a negative number.

Don't let negative influences define and limit the relationship with your man that you desire if there is nothing seriously hindering it and -if it is at all possible.

Chapter 25
Killing Him Softly

I was riding the bus home from work one day, and there was this man who was obviously drunk and/or high or on some type of drugs. Before we boarded the bus at the bus stop, he made an attempt to talk to just about every woman that he saw regardless of her race. He even tried to talk to this Asian woman and she was obviously afraid. Even with me, he tried to get my interest and attention, by telling me how pretty I was, but I did not entertain him. Anyway, he even tried to flirt with two young girls, but an older lady strongly voiced her opposition, about him trying with the girls. Eventually, the bus came and while getting his fare together to pay he said *"my girl didn't give me no monthly bus pass"*. Those of us, who had just witnessed his "attempts", erupted in laughter. But it was obvious that his "attempts" were him searching for happiness and/or a break from the drama at home.

Recently, I have been meeting guys who just aren't happy in their current relationships with their significant others, or families. They tend to find activities to engage in to get out the house and/ from the drama associated with being in their current relationships.

Many times we wonder why our men leave us and go places to get away from us. *Why do they take "brain breaks"?* Because we nag, argue and stress them. (A foolish child is a father's ruin, and a quarrelsome wife is like the constant dripping of a leaky roof. Proverbs 19:13) A man mentally doesn't want to deal with the anguish that we are putting him through. His heart doesn't want to be hurt, especially if he has finally trusted us enough and opened it up to us. *Ladies,* please stop making your man have to make unnecessary trips to stores, bars, gas stations, bus stops, parks, gyms, etc. just to get away from you. There may come a day when he may actually go and NOT come back… And unfortunately, there are *other* women who are willing to give him *other* activities to engage in like sex; affection; dating; hanging out; and various other stress relievers. Hopefully, he will be strong enough to withstand outside offers. But if it gets to the point where he no longer cares and/or is *fed* up, he may accept other offers. Some men may still try and *keep the peace* with you despite them not being happy especially if they have kids with you. They'll be there for them and not because he wants to be with you. Do you realize that the man you consider yourself in a relationship with, may be heavily drinking and smoking; and it could be your fault. He could be miserable with you, or the relationship; his job, or life in general. But he genuinely cares about you and may or may not know how to tell you because mentally his mind is not strong enough to. A man-your man could be using alcohol; sex with others; or drugs as self-medication and crying out for help; even though, a person is responsible for his or her own actions, decisions, and consequences.

Men are naturally and by instinct providers, who fight all day in the streets, and at work. He does all that he can throughout the day to make sure that home is ok, secure and safe. But at some point he needs to be able to relax, unwind and be relieved from life's pressures. His home should be different. If he is constantly in some type of battle, then when does he get peace? Where does he go to seek refuge? If he is taking care of the household and his responsibilities, then video games and watching sports should be the least of your *peeves* about him finally relaxing. You may get *your time* to relax and pamper yourself by getting manicures; pedicures; going to the spa; getting your hair done or simply by taking a relaxing bubble bath. But when does he get his turn to do the same? If he has to constantly be in anguish in the streets, against the world, and tormented with you?

What do you prefer - a healthy man, or a man who could be slowly committing suicide by drinking, smoking, and/or using drugs? Oh, and his drug of choice may not be weed; cocaine; alcohol; meth; heroine etc. it be other women…just something to think about.

Is your man really finding more contentment at work, with his boys, or at a bar, or avoiding you so that he can find some peace? Or does he prefer to be at home with you because that is where he has the most peace? If you can't answer "yes" to him wanting to be home with you, then you could be the reason that the *quality time* that you may desire to be spent by him with you, is at a bare minimum. What can you do different to increase your man's desire to want to spend time with you? Why don't you work on helping him live a long and productive life? Speak life into him by speaking positive things to him since *death and life are in the power of the tongue: and they that love it shall eat the fruit thereof* (Proverbs 18:21) through positive declarations, about how you appreciate him; love him; aren't expecting him to be your super hero etc. There may be times when you have to as Beyonce says *cater to him* by rubbing his back, shoulders, or feet (yes his feet); running him a soothing bath or something else to help him to relax. But most of all-give him a peaceful environment when at all possible and enjoy your life with *your man!*

Chapter 26
You Made It Easy
For the Clean Up Woman

Sometimes we as women take the man in our life for granted. Sometimes we are vindictive and spiteful, or just plain comfortable. Although, men tend to spoil us, we tend to get complicit in the goodness that they give us, and over the time of the course of the relationship we start change into spoiled brats. Some of us allow a man to give us more and more; then we want *more,* and then more and then more and more take them for granted. Then if something happens like them losing their job, getting a pay cut, having to better manage their money etc., and they can't spoil us anymore we get mad and change our attitude towards them. But rest assured, there is a solution to keep being able to maintain our being *spoiledness.* With the right attitude a man will try or make a way to show his lady that he appreciates her. But before I tell you how to keep getting spoiled, I have to tell you what will happen if you act too spoiled.

When a man no longer feels wanted, loved and appreciated there is a consequence that we as women may end up having to face. Her name is the *"Clean up Woman"*. She may be the woman who meets and exceeds his wants and needs emotionally, mentally, and physically, and she may even cook a meal for him and clean up after him too. She may begin as a good friend and/or confident but he will allow her to get closer and closer to his mind and to his heart until she enters into an intimate place in his heart. She may quickly get a promotion to the place which you once held-as his lady because you have become more self-absorbed with your own wants and needs instead of being willing to be your man's partner and meet his wants and needs. He will begin to feel hurt. Simply put…you have made it easy for another woman, to pick up the pieces of his heart. Every time you hurt him and break his heart, another woman is waiting with a broom, dust pan and *super glue*, to put the pieces of him back together. Picture it like this have you ever broken your favourite glass or coffee mug on the floor? You know, that glass or coffee mug that you love to drink out of every day? You may do whatever you can to salvage as many pieces of it as you can, but some of the pieces may still get swept up and thrown away. You use glue to glue it back together but over time the wear and tear on the glass/mug or it breaking again eventually causes you to have no choice but to throw it away.

A man's heart is like that glass or that mug. Once it is broken some of the pieces may get scattered, and if he feels as though you have thrown him and/or his heart away, he and his heart will leave you mentally, emotionally, and/or physically. The possibility of him returning a being back in a relationship with you is possible but it may take some time to get things back to even close to how they were before, because of his fear of his heart being broken again. The time of his return is similar to a "quick fix" using tape instead of permanent glue because your relationship has yet to be permanent or restored.

The remedy of another woman will be stronger than the *"tape"* that you used to temporarily fix what you kept messing up. In the beginning, there is a small amount of lead way because you may be able to still manipulate and confuse him emotionally while there are still cracks in his heart. But know that once the *"glue"* which she used dries, you are permanently dismissed from the opportunity to get him back. Eventually you have to accept the fact that you pushed him to that other woman, and it wasn't hard for her to be there waiting for him, because she is the type of woman whom he desired to have and build a relationship with anyway. You actually had potential, but you put your wants and needs first instead of having them run parallel with his and towards oneness. Now, I know that she could be "Miss Perfect" for now and may have *another side* to her, but that's not for you or me to worry about. If she does – that will be his problem –lol.

Anyway, in the beginning of your relationship with your man, you may have been the *Clean Up Lady*. Remember that *ex* that you stole your man from by being a shoulder to cry on? You were a rebound who used *tape* to get him. But once he realized that the grass wasn't greener on the other side and nothing more than artificial turf, he returned and may be better than ever, *TO HER (or the next "Clean up Woman"!* Remember earlier I mentioned Kyle? Well Kyle wife began as a *"Clean up Woman"*. When he and I somewhat broke up she acted as a shoulder to cry on even though she used manipulation to do it. See Kyle and she worked together and when he first introduced me to her and her then husband I sensed that she was attracted to Kyle and was unhappily married. Based on her looks and how she frequently called him. Anyway, this should explain why he attempted to return to me. She used a mental magnet to draw him personally away from me to her by focusing on his emotions and hurt by me. But once he realized that her antics were foul and superficial, her spell had worn off and he knew that he had to return and restart a relationship with me. Once a man deals with his main lady and his *Clean up Woman,* much like Kyle, your man has now had an experience with you or others, and is learning himself, his feelings and his needs. Contrary to what we think, a man doesn't want multiple women. He really does want just one whom he can love and cherish. Having to deal with the many emotions and more especially from multiple women confuses and eventually frustrates a man. It's easier for him to learn and master the relationship between himself and one spouse, than with multiple spouses. Again, a man wants to give one woman his *all.* Since I have been both the wife and *wifey,* this would be a good time to define the difference between the two.

A **GIRLFRIEND** is temporary. A **WIFEY** is the main girl but may not be the only girl. A **WIFE** is the one a man respects, honours and cherishes and his only one. Please repeat after me I mean please read aloud-I'm **WIFE** not **WIFEY** material. Why? A **WIFE** gets the **RING** and all of the benefits. A **WIFEY** gives up all the benefits but gets no ring. A female should not just desire to be a girlfriend or a wifey but the wife. Again it's a man's choice whether or not you are the one whom God says completes him, and if you are his missing rib!

Remember, in earlier chapters I mentioned how God opened up Adam and used one of Adam's ribs to create Eve? I hope by now you see how important this fact is and that it is embedded it in your psyche. A man only has two ribs and if he keeps giving them away how can or will he survive? Strive to be the one and only lady that he needs and wants in his life and not the one that he desires to have.

Once he's gone, you'll once again be alone except for the kids that you may have convinced him or someone else to give to you.

Don't settle for being the *"Clean up Woman"* be willing to get your hands dirty as you make your relationship work-so that you are the ONLY woman. Hopefully by the time you get to the end of this book you can answer to some degree *Oh! Is That Why I'm Still Single?"* But before you turn the pages and get to the Epilogue, relationship surveys etc. let me leave you with this thought based on a post I saw similar to this post on Tagged.com, which again is a website for meeting people. The message along with some of my additions basically says:

What if the person you never met, never talked to, never laid eyes on, never dated, never made love to, never hugged, never kissed, never smiled at, never held their hand, never walked arm in arm, never fell in love with…was the one you were supposed to be with?

The End for Now

Be on the lookout for part three of this trilogy…

Part 1:   *I Married Satan*

Part 2:   *Oh! Is that Why I'm Still Single?*

Part 3:

(I can't tell you yet because I do not know the title or its subject. I just know that God said that there will be a trilogy)

Epilogue

One day this metaphoric revelation came to me: years ago I wasn't truly ready for you because I was allowing little boys to play in the shallow end of my pool. Now I have learned that if I venture out further in the pool, that the pool gets deeper and only those who can swim will jump in. Some will be bold enough to jump off the diving board; but many less will reach the bottom. The pool discussed here is symbolic of **MY HEART**!

I didn't know or understand how deep true love really was until I continued to journey on through life. I had some relationships work (*I was able to swim*), and some fail (*they almost drowned me*). Some have tread water (*barely made it and the guys had fake motives in dealing with me*); some didn't put forth an effort and just tried to go along for the ride (*they drifted and floated through*). Some didn't put their *all* in it like I did (*they got their feet wet but they may, or may not have been dressed/prepared for the trip or the depth of my love that I was ready to give, so they never got completely in or fully committed*). But each and every experience brought me to a point where I finally learned what true love from a man, and more importantly God is, and how I should expect to receive it unconditionally.

True love waits – if God designed for you to be together. You will be with him. And if you do end up married, just know that as two elders at my church who are married Elder Marty and Karen, while sharing their testimony one Sunday, marriage affects more than just the two people who said "I do", it affects those around them as well.

If you picked us this book I believe that you have a desire to be married and God sees your heart. Stay in position.

I was working on the final edits of this book during our church wide fast. As the dates got closer to me finalizing this book, more and more revelations and information began to be spiritually downloaded to me. I had to keep paper and something to write with close by me. It seemed like every time I thought I was done-I wasn't and I had to add more content, which meant longer retypes and formatting. But hey, how do you eat an elephant? Answer: one bite at a time. The book finally got completed.

With that being said, let me leave you with this final thought. What God put together, let no man (or woman) come in between and destroy it. Once you get married and if things get ruff and you feel like quitting, remember that as Pastor Tony Brazelton said "Jesus is not just an example for us, He is an example of us." Jesus was resurrected from the dead and so can our marriage, relationships, thoughts and desires.

True love is imitated but never duplicated.

The reason that you may still be single
is because of your mindset.

Repeat after me…
I believe I receive

Acknowledgments

This book is actually my second book that I actually published. It is only by the grace of God that I am able to share my gift with you. I would have never imagined in a million times two years that I would see my name on the cover of a book. But it was all written in God's plan before I was even conceived. Lord God as always I thank you for being the head of my life, for being my strength and my passion!

To my mother Montrue Crawford. Wow there is so much that I could say but it would take up all of the pages of the book and more. The best way that I can sum it up is like this: I watched your struggles and your sacrifice for my brother and I, and I took notes. I hope and pray that I will grow to if even a quarter of the woman that you are. I love you and thank you for everything. To my brother and sisters: Tommy, Frankie and Chanel I love each of you individually and collectively. To my nephew AJ-*Áuntie loves her Pookie Butt* My fantabulous Uncle David…I just love you soooooo much.

God had already called home many famous and celebrity singers but he needed a dynamic musician so he called *home* my grandmother Montrue A. Cornish. If I started listing and explaining why I am grateful to her just this part alone would probably take up the rest of the book. I miss her like crazy!

To my *current Boo/Boo Thang* (wink), my heart, my love Milton Thomas Smith III. Thank you for giving me the biggest gift a man could ever give me-his heart. I cannot explain how awesome God's timing is. No sooner than I learn from and complete this book, my graduation present is you! I love you baby (please don't make me have to white this out wink).

Christina; Angie; Will; Jonathan; Marcel; LaBarbara; Beth and Vaughn; who are my fellow train riders. Thank you all for your conversations and your therapy sessions. I miss all the fun we had.

All of the media outlets thank you for the opportunities to introduce my projects to your audiences. Please continue pressing on in your ventures. See you at the top.

Some special mentions (not in any order):Karrie Proctor; FuShon Coleman; Darron Moore; Mari Jonas Zetino; Eric Thornes; Delone "Dojah" Matthews; Shantelle Willis; Que Dutton; Mondelle Pope; Denise Crumpton; Staci Rutherford; Ashley Newman; Maria Moore; Tish Smith; Rich Walker; Lavonne Dillard; Wanda Diggs; Corey Williams; Darnell Rogers; and Kimberly Simmons. Thank you all for pushing me and keeping me going.

To everyone who let me vent to them about my relationship/dating *goods* and *bads*.

To everyone who has read my previous works, sent words of encouragement (whether you read them or not), words cannot describe how much you mean to me. Thank you for everything. And an even bigger thank you goes out to those who encouraged me or cheered me up and you didn't even know it.

Wow, I can't forget about my Facebook, Onyx, Twitter, Linkedin and various other website families. Honestly, if I didn't interact with you all on a regular basis, my life would probably be a lot duller lol.

If you feel that I should have included you by name please insert it here ________________________________.

Everyone last one of you is

FANTABULOUS and ROCK!

References

http://en.wikipedia.org/wiki/Oxytocin

www.google.com

http://www.psychologytoday.com/blog/the-sexual-continuum/201112/how-often-do-men-and-women-think-about-sex

The scriptures used came mainly from me using Google to search for the subject matter, and then scrolling down through the search results. I would then click on the link to the appropriate scripture, based on the scripture matching what I was searching for.

Extras to further help you with answering…

Oh!
Is That Why I'm Still Single?

Please use this next session to help find out if you are still single because of:

Choice

Past hurts

Unhealthy attractions

What did or did not work in past relationships

Waiting for your Boaz

Fear of commitment

Too picky

Too busy

Fear of intimacy

You have too many rules

Low self esteem

Fear of competition

Too isolated

Too routine

Defenses up

Negative attitude

Extras to Help You Answer Why You Are Still Single

ABOUT
YOU

Extras to Help You Answer Why You Are Still Single

Exercise

In the space below or on a separate sheet of paper or in your journal, place your answers to the following questions:

ABOUT YOU

- List five reasons (in order) of why you believe that you are single (or unmarried even if you are divorced)

    1. ____________________________

    2. ____________________________

    3. ____________________________

    4. ____________________________

    5. ____________________________

- Now (without showing anyone your list) ask five of your **FEMALE** friends and associates, why they believe that you are still single. This is merely their opinion and may or may not line up to your reasons. Remember they are not you. List the top five answers below.

    1. ____________________________

    2. ____________________________

    3. ____________________________

    4. ____________________________

    5. ____________________________

Extras to Help You Answer Why You Are Still Single

- Repeat question number two, but this time, ask five **MALE** friends/associates. List the top five answers below.

    1. _______________________________
    2. _______________________________
    3. _______________________________
    4. _______________________________
    5. _______________________________

Any similarities (or overlapping) between answers given by your male and female friends? How do the answers compare with the reasons that you listed in question one?

____
____
____
____
____
____
____
____

- Not what can be done differently on your part?

____
____
____
____
____

Extras to Help You Answer Why You Are Still Single

ABOUT
YOUR MATE

Extras to Help You Answer Why You Are Still Single

If you are currently dating, create a Dating Checklist about your **<u>current</u>** mate. In the space below, on a separate sheet of paper or in your journal, place your answers to the following:

On the left side list all of the good qualities and positive attributes about your mate. Include what you love and adore about them. On the right list all of the bad qualities and negative attributes, as well as what you do not like about him.

<u>**Good Qualities**</u>   <u>**Bad Qualities**</u>

Which list is the longest?

____

Are their some items on the list that are irrelevant or petty
and could be taken off?

____
____
____
____
____

How can you balance the list?

____
____
____
____
____
____

If the bad outweighs the good-why are you still with him?

____
____
____
____
____
____

An Awesome Relationship Survey...

I sent this survey out to a few men whom I have gone out with and/or had a relationship with. The responses were somewhat surprising…especially when they admitted fault and stated that they wanted to try our relationship again…this could be very beneficial to you to (1) get honest answers, and (2) realize that you are not as bad of a person as you allowed yourself to be made to believe that you are; especially if you are still friends with an ex.

Relationship Survey

I have chosen you because you have been one of the most significant, influential and memorable relationships in my life.

<u>Please be as specific as you can</u> about your memories. If you prefer to you can audio record the answer to these questions instead of writing or typing them.

1. Do you remember being in a relationship with me
    or could it be defined as something else? If
    something else please explain.

2. Do you remember how we met? (i.e. where we
    were, did someone introduce us, was it in person or
    somewhere else?) Please explain.

3. How long generally did our relationship or
    experiences with one another last with one another
    (few weeks, few months, few days, few hours
    etc.?) Any insight to why the short or long time
    duration?

4. Why did you believe or feel was the reason for our
    break up or us to stop dealing with one another?

5. Could you see yourself being with me again now
    that you see the type of woman that I have grown
    and matured into?

6. What were some things that I could have done
    different, better etc. to maintain a healthy
    relationship with you? What do/did I need to
    change?

7. Did we ever have sex? If so, did this contribute to
    us not having a successful relationship and/or our
    break up? Did I act different or strange or stupid
    afterward? Did you?

8. Were there any issues in me that you picked up
    on/scared you off etc.? Age, immaturity etc.

9. Were there any issues, situations or things that you
    were dealing with which made our relationship or

encounters with one another not work?

10. Other thoughts/comments/suggestions?

Now review the answers that he/they gave you.

- Are his/their answers applicable to you?

- Do they really make sense?

- Do you have a clear and concise understanding of the answers?

- Are there changes that you are willing to make based on the answers?

- Are there characteristics about you that you want to keep the same and don't believe that you should change?

- Are the answers that you received-THE REASON THAT YOU MAY STILL BE UNMARRIED?

Special Offers

25% off the purchase of

I Married Satan (paperback book)

With proof of purchase of ***Oh! Is That Why I'm Still Single***. This offer is valid exclusively towards the purchase of *I Married Satan* from *Fire and Words Publishing*™. Only valid on mail order and website purchases from *Fire and Words Publishing*™. Must provide copy of receipt from purchase, with the name of the retailer and date in order to qualify for the discount. Discount request must be presented at the time of purchase of *I Married Satan*. One discount coupon is valid per purchase. Cannot be combined with any other offer.

or

1 book $15-2 books $20

Show proof that you purchased this book for the full retail price of $14.95 and get ***I Married Satan*** for only *$5.00* from *Fire and Words Publishing*™. Must provide copy of receipt from purchase, with the name of the retailer and date in order to qualify for the discount. Discount request must be presented at the time of purchase of *I Married Satan*. One discount coupon is valid per purchase.

Cannot be combined with any other offer.

We reserve the right, at our sole discretion, to change, modify or otherwise alter these terms and conditions at any time.

About the Author:

LaDonna M. Smith

LaDonna M. Smith is a native of Maryland. However she has also briefly resided in Philadelphia and Indianapolis. She has worked many paid and unpaid positions in broadcast, print, media and other professional positions throughout the DC/MD/VA areas (better known as the DMV) including Baltimore.

Although she has always had a passion for writing and would as a child get in trouble for staying up late past her bed time writing, she began writing her first book *I Married Satan* in 2007. The book began as a magazine article to get revenge on her *husband* but the book ended up causing LaDonna to do introspection and forgive her ex-*husband*, instead of seeking further revenge. It was later submitted and rejected by a publisher. LaDonna began selling copies of her book to friends and family and soon she had her first book signing (May 26,2011) where she sold 26 books in less than four hours. This encouraged LaDonna to continue to write, create and produce quality info-tainment products and before long she was creating her other upcoming books; writing for online magazines; creating, hosting and executing live events; and production for various other media outlets, to include radio broadcast. LaDonna has also host and produced her own tv show (*The Mix TV Show);* radio show (*The Mix Radio Show);* and is the owner of her own magazine (*G.R.A.Y. Magazine).*

Additionally, she has served on the Board of Directors as the Events Coordinator Black Writer's Guild of Maryland; and as President and Vice President of the Maryland Writer's Association (Baltimore Chapter).

If you ever want to know what LaDonna M. Smith is currently working on-Google/Bing her name.

To reach LaDonna, please contact Fire and Words Publishing™ on (443) 267-8698

(general) fireandwords@gmail.com

(for media events and speaking engagements)

ldmsevents@gmail.com

Twitter: twitter.com/ladonnamsmith

Facebook: LaDonna M. Smith

Order Form

Fire and Words Publishing™-
A subsidiary of Philatonian Productions™
(443) 267-8698· fireandwords@gmail.com

________ I Married Satan (paperback)　　　　$14.95

________ I Married Satan (ebook)　　　　$9.95

________ Oh! Is That Why I'm Still Single　　　　$14.95
(paperback)

________ Oh! Is That Why I'm Still Single　　　　$9.95
(ebook)

CHILDREN'S BOOK

Hannah's Song: A Musical Approach to Potty Training
　　　Coming Soon!

Shipping and handling (USA) via USPS mail　　　　$4.00
Total for 1 book (adult-USA)　　　　$18.95

Please contact us for Canada and International Prices

Please print:
Name: ____

ID # (if incarcerated) ____________________________

Address: _______________________________________

City: ________________________________　State: ________

Zip code: ____________________________

Special discounts for book clubs and bulk orders-call (443) 267-8698 for information. For mail orders we accept money orders only.

Order Form

Fire and Words Publishing™-
A subsidiary of Philatonian Productions™
(443) 267-8698·fireandwords@gmail.com

______ I Married Satan (paperback) $14.95

______ I Married Satan (ebook) $9.95

______ Oh! Is That Why I'm Still Single $14.95
            (paperback)

______ Oh! Is That Why I'm Still Single $9.95
            (ebook)

CHILDREN'S BOOK

Hannah's Song: A Musical Approach to Potty Training
       Coming Soon!

Shipping and handling (USA) via USPS mail $4.00
Total for 1 book (adult-USA) $18.95

Please contact us for Canada and International Prices

Please print:
Name: ____

ID # (if incarcerated) ________________________________

Address: ______________________________________

City: _____________________________ State: _________

Zip code: __________________________

Special discounts for book clubs and bulk orders-call (443) 267-8698 for information. For mail orders we accept money orders only.

Order Form

Fire and Words Publishing™-
A subsidiary of Philatonian Productions™
(443) 267-8698·fireandwords@gmail.com

______ I Married Satan (paperback) $14.95

______ I Married Satan (ebook) $9.95

______ Oh! Is That Why I'm Still Single $14.95
(paperback)

______ Oh! Is That Why I'm Still Single $9.95
(ebook)

CHILDREN'S BOOK

Hannah's Song: A Musical Approach to Potty Training
       Coming Soon!

Shipping and handling (USA) via USPS mail $4.00
Total for 1 book (adult-USA) $18.95

Please contact us for Canada and International Prices

Please print:
Name: ____

ID # (if incarcerated) ____________________________________

Address: ____

City: __________________________________ State: ________

Zip code: _______________________

Special discounts for book clubs and bulk orders-call (443) 267-8698 for information. For mail orders we accept money orders only.

Order Form

Fire and Words Publishing™-
A subsidiary of Philatonian Productions™
(443) 267-8698·fireandwords@gmail.com

_______ I Married Satan (paperback) $14.95

_______ I Married Satan (ebook) $9.95

_______ Oh! Is That Why I'm Still Single $14.95
(paperback)

_______ Oh! Is That Why I'm Still Single $9.95
(ebook)

CHILDREN'S BOOK

Hannah's Song: A Musical Approach to Potty Training
Coming Soon!

Shipping and handling (USA) via USPS mail $4.00
Total for 1 book (adult-USA) $18.95

Please contact us for Canada and International Prices

Please print:
Name: ____

ID # (if incarcerated) ____________________________

Address: ______________________________________

City: _______________________________ State: ________

Zip code: ____________________

Special discounts for book clubs and bulk orders-call (443) 267-8698 for information. For mail orders we accept money orders only.